FOREST MANAGEMENT GUIDE BEST PRACTICES IN A CLIMATE-CHANGED WORLD

A Resilient Forest Publication

By Catriona M. Glazebrook, esq.

J.D., M.S. in Resource Management & Administration

Note: While this Guide highlights California in some instances, the scientific information contained herein and policy suggestions have application to forest management in other states (especially in the western US) and internationally, especially in those regions impacted by drought, extreme heat, and forest fires.Note: While this Guide highlights California in some instances, the scientific information contained herein and policy suggestions have application to forest management in other states (especially in the western US) and internationally, especially in those regions impacted by drought, extreme heat, and forest fires.

ISBN: 979-8-218-32849-8

Contents

INTRODUCTION

"We cannot protect the Earth's biodiversity without protecting our forests. They harbor most of the world's terrestrial biodiversity and support food security, jobs, and livelihoods for millions of people. Conservation, restoration, and sustainable use are key to curbing deforestation and protecting the world's forests into the future."
– Will Simonson, Senior Programme Officer, Climate Change and Biodiversity,UNEP-WCMC

Forests are our most vital natural climate allies due to the tremendous "ecological values" they bring, including carbon sequestration, oxygen production, atmospheric moisture, shade, wildlife habitat, and more. The International Panel on Climate Change has indicated that land use, including deforestation, is climate change's second most pressing driver (IPCC, 2019). In addition, The Glasgow Declaration, signed by over 140 countries, calls for halting and reversing forest loss and land degradation by 2030 (UN Climate Change Conference, 2021). While trees and forest lands have been declining steadily for hundreds of years, they are being more rapidly decimated by climate change impacts, fires, and mismanagement.

Canada broke the record in late June for wildfire smoke emissions released in a single year when wildfires began raging in May, long before the fire season, and are still burning with fervor. More than 42 million acres have burned across Canada. The total wildfire emissions

for 2023 are estimated to be almost 410 megatons, the highest on record for Canada by a wide margin, according to the Copernicus Atmosphere Monitoring Service dataset, which provides information on the location, intensity, and estimated emission of wildfires around the world.

CAMS senior scientist Mark Parrington said, "As temperatures keep increasing and dry conditions become more long-term, the chances of experiencing devastating wildfires like those in Canada are increasing," Significant wildfires also impacted Russia's boreal forests. In contrast, devastating wildfires were experienced in Greece, Spain, Portugal, and Maui, Hawaii. While the global death toll due to wildfires surpassed 3,000, a 2017 study published in Environmental Health Perspectives estimated that nearly 1,500 deaths in Europe can be attributed to wildfire pollution alone.

Given the devastating harm from forest fires, it is understandable why forest managers, policymakers, and the public are calling to cut and thin trees. Yet, this is not a solution and does more harm than good. As will be shown via peer review studies and more, thinning forest lands and over-cutting native trees are making things worse.

Forest thinning exacerbates climate change since logging emits more than five times what wildfires and tree mortality from insects combined emit (Harris et al., 2016). Commercial thinning

This is just the tip of the iceberg, as forests and trees are not only Not our enemy when it comes to climate change, they are humankind's greatest ally. This is because plants created our atmosphere, terraformed our planet, and continue to play a critical role in maintaining the ecological balance of our world. That balance is desperately needed now.

This guide provides important scientific information often overlooked in management decisions and suggests alternatives to dominant and antiquated forest management methods and perspectives.

Forests In Peril

Forests are in peril. More than 20,000 tree species are threatened with extinction. Since 1990, the world has lost a billion acres of forest. The world is estimated to have lost 1/3 of its total forest lands. For example, the sacred Hawaiian Ohi'a tree, a flowering evergreen that covers 80% of the state's canopy that sustains birds and insects found nowhere else in the world, is being wiped out by a dangerous fungus. In Canada, mountain pine beetles are eating through entire forests. In 2015 alone, the beetles felled over 730 million cubic meters of pine trees in British Columbia. B.C. is a major exporter of wood to the U.S. and it's expected that the beetles alone will destroy 55% of marketable pine trees by 2020. Eucalyptus trees in Australia are also severely declining from cutting for agricultural purposes, pathogens, fire, and pollution. It is estimated that globally, these trees have declined by no less than 30%.[1]

Climate change and extreme heat are a leading cause of declines in tree species and forest lands. In extreme heat, even rain does little good to moisturize the soil. Just as damp soil in a hot oven dries out quickly, so does rain; it just evaporates away. Then there is simply not enough soil moisture left to support the roots of plants.

Besides, ten times the number of trees are being consumed by fire than just ten years ago.[i]Trees cannot handle the increased heat and unusual precipitation patterns global warming brings. In contrast, pests that harm trees, like the pine beetle, seem to thrive in the Earth's warmer, unnatural condition.

In California, the loss of 33 million acres (1/3 of the state's forest lands (CA.gov, 2020). Has occurred due to unprecedented drought, agriculture, fires, insect infestation, diseases, and other causes (USDA, 2019).

Called the "worst epidemic of tree mortality in modern history" by former

---

[1] William R.L. Anderegg, Jeffrey M. Kane, and Leander D.L. Anderegg, "Consequences of widespread tree mortality triggered by drought and temperature stress," Nature Climate Change 3 (2013): 30-36.

Governor Jerry Brown, this statewide tree die-off is already causing a dramatic loss in biodiversity (CA.gov, 2015). Plants and trees are the foundation for other life forms, not to mention the providers of 98% of the oxygen in the atmosphere (FAO, 2022). How do we protect our forests and communities from these threats? According to traditional thinking and present policies, the answer seems to be forest thinning: cutting down trees to reduce "fuel" for fires. Government agencies and many certified foresters follow this view. From 2014 to 2018, federal agencies harvested 301 to 400 million board feet of wood each year in California (Riddle, 2019). Forestry agencies have pledged in 2020 to thin out 1 million acres of forest each year by 2025 to reduce fires (U.S. Forest Service and State of California, 2020).

However, this strategy does not stop fires but destroys biodiversity and promotes fire-friendly conditions. For example, cutting and thinning forests causes hotter and faster fires across the Western United States (Bradley, Hanson, & DellaSala, 2016). The primary methods used in forest management do nothing to address the direct causes of the fires: climate change and human-caused burns.

Increasing temperatures, drought, UV radiation, and worsening soil values impact forest lands like never before. In addition, people start 90 percent or more of the fires intentionally or by accident via debris burning, campfires, lit cigarettes, and more (Insurance Information Institute, 2021). We must pay more attention on stopping fires before they start.

We must recognize the root causes of tree and forest declines and limit wildfires by stopping them at their source. Caring for our forests supports critical ecosystems and brings climate resilience.

Forests Are Essential Earth Systems

"Trees are essential for global ecosystems and the global economy. We treat them as an inexhaustible natural resource. Still, we need to urgently improve the management of trees for the supply of timber and sustainably manage tree diversity for the benefit of all communities."
~ Sara Oldfield, Co-Chair Global Tree Specialist Group (Oldfield et al., 2022)

Trees are the largest and longest-lived organisms on the planet. They constitute the framework of ecosystems, provide habitat for other creatures, and even create their own weather. Half of the world's known animal and plant species rely on trees for their habitat. Forests contain approximately 75% of bird species and 68% of the world's mammal species and are home to over 10 million species of invertebrates. Forest-dependent species have already declined by around 53% since 1970 due to the loss of trees.

Trees have intrinsic value and hold significant cultural significance. They provide aesthetic value and recreation, strengthening community relations, cultural connections, spirituality, and a sense of place. Many indigenous communities depend on trees for cultural identity, heritage, and knowledge, as particular tree species are linked with tribal identities and customs.

In addition, the Intergovernmental Panel on Climate Change has identified protecting old-growth forests as one of the biggest game-changers for addressing global warming. According to the Panel, *"While some response options have immediate impacts, others take decades to deliver measurable results. Examples of response options with immediate impacts include the conservation of high-carbon ecosystems such as…forests"* (IPCC, 2019).

In a climate-changed world, the many services mature trees add—including carbon sequestration, oxygen production, shade, and more—are critical to maintaining. However, under California's current wildfire mitigation strategy, which involves thinning five million acres of forest land over five years, hundreds of millions of trees will be removed (U.S. Forest Service & the State of California, 2020). This means we will lose the valuable services trees and forests provide.

A thinned forest routinely has far fewer large trees since the more giant trees are generally the first to be removed during selective logging operations (Shwartz, 2005). This is because it's more profitable to cut and sell larger trees. Yet, getting rid of the older trees causes the greatest harm.

Older trees tend to be more fire-resistant because of their thick bark; some are decades and centuries old and have survived many fires. Mature trees also provide the above "services" at much greater rates, equating to a higher ecological value than newly planted saplings. It takes many years (30-40 at a minimum) before a newly planted or grown sapling can provide similar levels of oxygen, moisture, shade, habitat, and food for wildlife. Thus, by cutting old-growth and mature trees, we are losing the beneficial services trees provide for almost an entire generation. In a climate-changed world, we cannot afford to wait that long.

The most significant change in global temperature has occurred in the last 40 years (Lindsey & Dahlman, 2022). Climate change is damaging ecosystems and communities at an accelerating pace. The rate of warming since 1981 is more than twice that of the previous 100 years! The earth's temperature has warmed at 32 degrees °F per decade, with 2021 being the sixth warmest year on record based on NOAA's temperature data (Lindsey & Dahlman, 2022). At the same time, we are on track to surpass the 1.5 °C Paris Agreement threshold before the century is over (United Nations News, 2022).

This trajectory makes protecting mature trees for their vital values—carbon sequestration, oxygen production, moisture, and shade—vital in proactive mitigation. With that, it is crucial to understand the significantly greater values mature trees provide NOW to the environment compared to the values that saplings (newly planted trees) provide.

This trajectory makes protecting mature trees for their vital values—carbon sequestration, oxygen production, moisture, and shade—vital in proactive mitigation. With that, it is crucial to understand the significantly greater values mature trees provide NOW to the

environment compared to the values that saplings (newly planted trees) provide.

Carbon Sequestration

Trees are vital because of their continuous carbon uptake. It is necessary to recognize that mature trees sequester much more carbon than saplings. A Nature study examined 673,046 trees of 403 different species from around the world and found that for the majority of species, "mass growth rate increases continuously with tree size. Thus, large, old trees do not act simply as senescent carbon reservoirs but actively fix large amounts of carbon compared to smaller trees…" (Stephenson et al., 2014).

A study of 48 undisturbed primary or mature secondary forest plots worldwide discovered that the most significant 1 percent of trees in the U.S. accounted for around 30 percent of forest biomass (Lutz et al., 2018). The difference in biomass of larger, mature trees is critical in understanding their differences in carbon sequestration because the more significant the biomass, the greater the carbon sequestration.

U.S. temperate and boreal forests remove enough atmospheric carbon to reduce national annual net emissions by 11 percent. However, there is "potential for much more rapid atmospheric CO2 removal rates and biological carbon sequestration by intact and older forests" (Moomaw et al., 2019).

Reducing mature trees to replace them with saplings dramatically decreases carbon removal rates. It makes achieving the carbon sequestration rates necessary for timely climate change mitigation impossible.

Atmospheric Moisture

Trees equal water. Depending upon age, type, and size, trees absorb 10 to 150 gallons of water daily, but less than 5 percent remains in the tree for growth (Purdue University Extension, 2021). A substantial amount of water is released through transpiration from the stomata of leaves during photosynthesis.

Trees and forests vastly improve atmospheric conditions, with transpiration accounting for nearly all

local atmospheric moisture (Sternberg et al., 1997). On average, a mature 60-plus-year-old tree (Note variation depending upon species and health) can transpire roughly 100 gallons of water daily. As for smaller trees, a one-year-old tree will only produce 1-3 gallons of water per day. This is why preserving our mature trees is so important.

If half of the trees in a forest are mature trees, then thinning five million acres of forest land, as suggested in California's current wildfire mitigation plan, we will remove daily atmospheric contribution of about 53,125,000,000 gallons of water, with a total loss of 96,923,125,000,000 gallons over a five year period—approximately 2.62 times the amount of water that Lake Tahoe holds (United

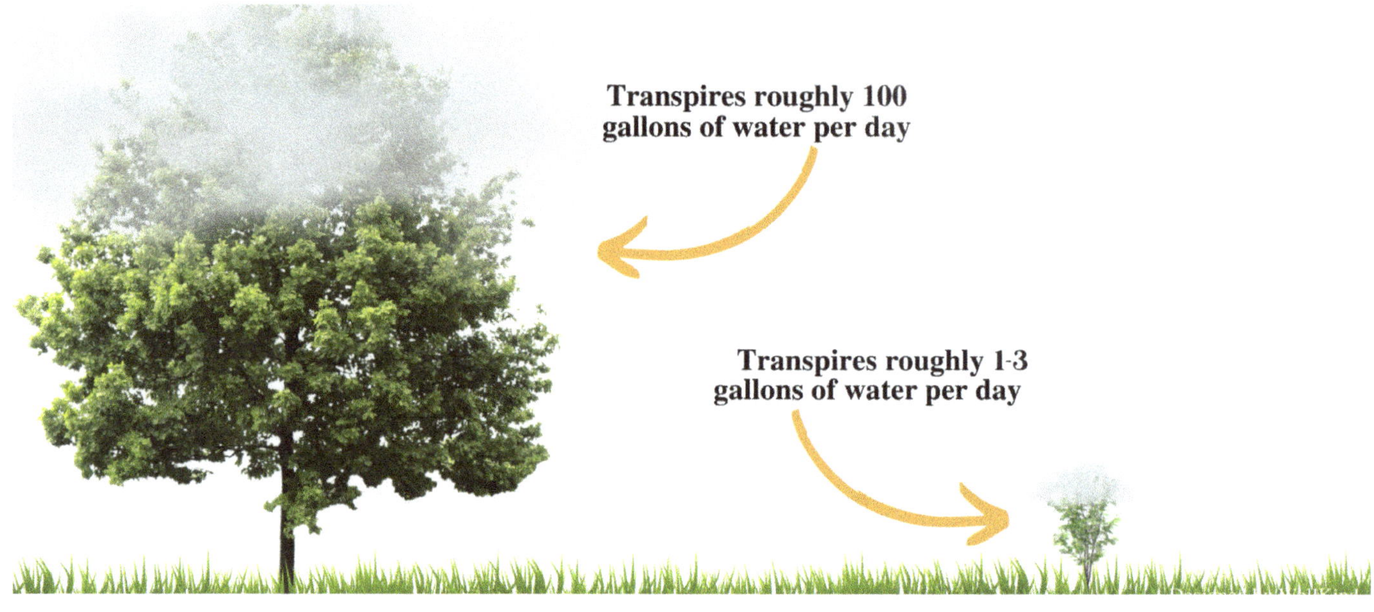

States Forest Service, 2016).

High atmospheric moisture levels have been proven to slow the spread of wildfires while, conversely, dry conditions allow for faster fire movement (Ferguson et al., 2013). On a regional scale, the importance of forests in maintaining atmospheric conditions is immense, especially when faced with situations brought about by climate change.

If half of the trees in a forest are mature trees, then thinning five million acres of forest land will remove daily atmospheric contribution of about 53,125,000,000 gallons of water, with a total loss of 96,923,125,000,000 gallons over five years—approximately 2.62 times the

amount of water that Lake Tahoe holds (United States Forest Service, 2016).

Though they cover only 20 percent of California, forests provide 65 percent of California's water (Swaffar, 2016). An average acre of Californian forest contains around 170 trees (Jakobs, 2020). Thus, the new state laws allowing the cutting of 5 million acres of forest lands over five years will result in a total loss of 96,923,125,000,000 gallons of water.

The local results of this moisture drawdown will be significant. A Forest Ecology and Management study studied microclimate data over five years and concluded that thinning and burning dramatically increased air temperature and dryness (Ma et al., 2010). It will further increase forests' susceptibility to wildfire.

Furthermore, trees regulate the water cycle. Forest watersheds create 75 percent of the freshwater on the planet (Millennium Ecosystem Report, 2005). Disrupting the water cycle can lead to decreases in crucial rainfall.

Oxygen

Mature trees produce and release significantly more significant amounts of oxygen into the atmosphere than saplings. On average, a tree will produce 260 pounds of oxygen throughout its lifetime (Environment Canada). A tree's total amount of oxygen depends on its total leaf area. Mature trees typically have bigger leaves, with one study finding that the site "is generally higher for upper canopy leaves of adult trees than for saplings, especially in temperate deciduous trees" (Thomas & Winner, 2002). Because mature trees typically have larger leaves, they photosynthesize more and produce more significant quantities of oxygen

Weather

Forests drive weather patterns and create rain. In a single day, the rainforest produces 20 billion metric tons of water released into the air and travels on airflow currents in the atmosphere (Amazon Aid Foundation, n.d.). To put things in perspective, this "invisible river" manages as much water as almost 50,000 Itaipu Dams, the second largest hydroelectric plant in the world.

The atmospheric river also creates worldwide weather patterns that all life needs and brings nutrients to oceans to feed microscopic life that the marine biodiversity depends upon for survival.

The ability of forests to attract clouds, pull water vapor from out at sea towards them, and release chemicals into the atmosphere to cause rain are all processes that forests provide. This is why trees are the answer to addressing drought conditions and sequestering carbon out of the atmosphere.

Shade, Ground Level Cooling, and Protection from UV

As the earth warms and is subjected to higher UV radiation, the protective cooling effect of shade is becoming more critical. Shade is crucial in preserving soil moisture and protecting plant animal and human life from harmful UV radiation.

Larger canopies of mature trees cast more shade than saplings due to their longer branches and larger leaves, reducing temperatures beneath and near them. Forest thinning of mature trees causves higher temperature increases on the ground and soil below.

The hotter the temperature, the drier the soil. Because trees predominantly absorb mvoisture from the soil, when that soil is dry, the forest's water source is gone. The result is simple: increased tree mortality rates and decreased forest health (Vose et al., 2016). In conjunction with warming air temperatures, dry soil substantially contributes to an overall shift toward drier environmental conditions—regardless of future increases in rainfall (Fisher et al., 2019).

Further, thick over-story cover stymies and slows the growth of understory vegetation–a standard vehicle for fire–by light deprivation. Removing shade-giving trees leads to accelerated growth of ground fuels that can make wildfires more intense (Robbins, 2015). A dense canopy of mature trees enables trees to maintain moisture further into fire seasons, decreasing fire potential.

vegetation–a standard vehicle for fire–by light deprivation. Removing shade-giving trees leads to accelerated growth of ground fuels that can make wildfires more intense (Robbins, 2015). A dense canopy of mature trees enables trees to maintain moisture further into fire seasons, decreasing fire potential.

The relationship is discernible: clear-cut, thinned, and heavily managed forest lands allow more direct sunlight to reach the ground to heat and dry the soil, while dense mature forests cast more shade and provide a cooling effect on the ground and soil below.

Biodiversity

In 2020, tens of thousands of birds were seen literally "falling out of the sky" in New Mexico, Colorado, Texas, Arizona, and Nebraska, as reported by The Guardian (Weston, 2020). According to the USGS, eighty percent of these birds had died from starvation.

Biologist Martha Desmond at New Mexico State University found that the birds "became so emaciated they had to turn to wasting their major flight muscles. This means that this isn't something that happened overnight." She points to the Southwest's long-term drought and the resulting lack of insects and berries as a major cause for this tragic loss of birds.

Birds depend on insects for survival. Each year, birds eat between 400 to 500 million tons of insects (Nyffeler et al., 2018). Ninety-six percent of all terrestrial bird species raise their young on insects. For example, feeding one clutch of chickadees takes more than 5,000 caterpillars (Lott, 2020)!

With climate change and deforestation, insects—and the birds that depend on them—are in jeopardy. In 2019, scientists found that 40 percent of all insect species are declining globally, and a third are endangered (Sánchez-Bayo and Wyckhuys, 2019). Researchers at the National Academy of Science report that we are losing 10-20 percent of all insects every decade (Wagner et al., 2021).

Along with fires, droughts, and other factors, they list deforestation as a major cause of these declines. Other researchers have identified that older forests are vital to protect, as they contain the highest diversity of insect species, some of which can only survive around old-growth trees (Sugar, 2000). Forests are critical integrated ecosystems that harbor most of the Earth's terrestrial biodiversity. Forests contain 60,000 different tree species, 80 percent of amphibian species, 75 percent of bird species, and 68 percent of the world's mammal species (FAO & UNEP, 2020). When forests are destroyed by cutting or fire, this puts in motion severe biodiversity losses locally and globally. Forest wildlife globally has declined by 53 percent since 1970 (World Wildlife Fund, 2019).

California lost over one million acres of natural habitat in the last twenty years, including 90 percent of coastal and inland wetlands, 99 percent of riparian zones, and 99 percent of our native grasslands (Gutierrez, 2020; California Native Grassland Association, 2021). Consequently, all native species have diminished by 20 percent in the state (Gutierrez, 2020), with the highest extinction rates in mammals and birds

(Stokstad, 2019).

One in four mammals are threatened with extinction; even more, Fifty-two percent of mammal populations are declining (Biello, 2008). With roughly 30 percent of California's species threatened by extinction (California Department of Fish and Wildlife, 2019), scientists predict it will take millions of years for mammals to recover from this biodiversity crisis naturally. However, scientists believe that by prioritizing such diversity in mammals, "we could save billions of years of unique evolutionary history and the important ecological functions they may represent" (Davis et al., 2018).

Believing that we can plant saplings to replace mature trees' "natural values" fails to consider that insects and wildlife cannot wait multiple generations to reproduce. We cannot afford to cut large, mature trees now and wait half a decade for new trees to provide biodiversity benefits. By doing so, we are pushing insects and wildlife species, already in jeopardy, to the brink.

Forest Management Needs to Address Present Planetary Conditions

As discussed in more detail, fire is only one of the many hazards forests face today. Drought, insect infestations, UV radiation, and other factors are killing off entire forests in several states and across the globe. It is estimated that 30 percent of trees worldwide are at risk of extinction (BGCI, 2021). In California, the U.S. Forest Service has recorded the deaths of over 129 million trees on 8.9 million acres since 2014 (U.S. Forest Service, 2017).

A significant factor is drought. From 2012 to 2014, California experienced its worst drought in 1,200 years (Griffin & Anchukaitis, 2014). In 2021, the state re-entered drought status (Sheffield, 2022). During prolonged dryness and drought periods, tree growth declines, mortality rates rise to 20 percent, pathogen and pest susceptibility increases, and seed production falls (Vose et al., 2016). If drought is prolonged, photosynthesis may shut down while root damage and loss can occur (Hartmann et al., 2022).

A new study published in Nature found that drought has pushed almost a quarter of Earth's best-protected forests to a point where even a minor drought or heat wave could tip them into catastrophic decline (Forzieri et al., 2022). Drought also makes trees more susceptible to other harms, such as:

UV Damage

In high enough concentrations, UV can damage DNA and sterilize and burn plants, hindering metabolic processes such as photosynthesis and carbon sequestration (Climate Policy Watcher, 2022). Drought-stricken trees are less able to fend off UV damage.

Loss of Biodiversity

North America has lost three billion birds since 1970 (Rosenberg et al., 2019). With the loss of birds comes a loss of critical providers of natural fertilizers that enrich the soil for trees and keep some moisture in place. Drought-ridden and weakened trees are less able to manage with lower soil nutrients and moisture.

Pests and Diseases

Under drought conditions, trees lose their ability to defend themselves from pests like pine bark beetles, killing millions of trees in California (CALFIRE, 2017). Researchers warn that beetles will kill 35 to 40 percent more ponderosa pines for each additional degree Celsius that Earth warms (Robbins et al., 2021).

Declining Regeneration Rates

Further highlighting the need to conserve forests is that fires have become so intense that it is harder for groves to regenerate after burns. Scientists from the U.S. Forest Service and U.C. Davis examined 14 burned areas through 10 national forests in California, and they concluded that recent wildfires have killed an innumerable amount of mature, seed-producing trees (Welch et al., 2016). UV radiation also sterilizes some trees and/or reduces their fertility rate

.

The lack of seeds makes it much harder for the forests to grow back. Forty-three percent of the nearly 1,500 plots studied showed no natural conifer regeneration. In addition, areas where trees don't grow back are susceptible to larger wildfires in the future, as dead, fallen trees, lost air moisture, and warmer temperatures fuel catastrophic blazes (Chung, 2017).

New saplings also have a harsher environment to establish themselves than trees that started growing 100 years ago, before weather changes. Thus, newly planted trees have a lower survivability rate. Those that survive are weakened by drought and other inhospitable conditions (Gee, 2021).

These are only a few examples of the threats that trees face today.

Since 2020, climbing temperatures and fires have resulted in the loss of 13 to 19 percent of the entire population of the iconic Sequoias and California's coastal redwoods, both tree species that tourists travel from all parts of the world to see, are in danger of being lost. Even California's "Methuselah tree," a bristlecone pine thought to be the oldest tree in the world, is threatened by drought and pine bark beetles (Kaplan, 2022). Our forestry agencies must recognize that the confluence of these threats makes it all the more critical that we conserve what trees we can, emphasizing these iconic and ancient trees.

We can no longer apply traditional forest management techniques developed in a different era. Applying forest management policies and practices that address these new conditions is critical.

The Land Feeds the Animals & the Animals Feed the Land

Loss of Wildlife Biodiversity Affects Forests

There is overwhelming evidence that biodiversity is being destroyed at a rate unprecedented in human history. In the last 50 years, two-thirds of wildlife species have declined (World Wildlife Fund, 2020). In addition, in 2019, an intergovernmental panel of scientists concluded that one million species (500,000 animals and plants and 500,000 insects) are threatened with extinction, some within decades (Briggs, 2020).

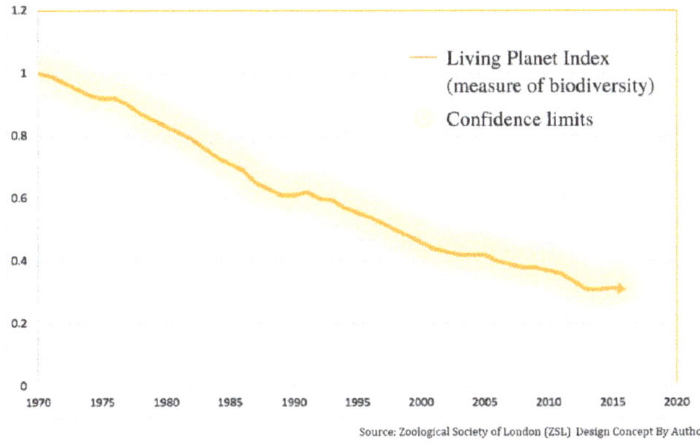

Source: Zoological Society of London (ZSL). Design Concept By Author

Nutrients are vital compounds used to sustain plant life and growth. Without them, growth stalls, plant tissue dies, and leaves yellow (Shrivastav et al., 2020). Nitrogen, for example, is one of life's most important and primary nutrients since it is an essential component of many biomolecules and regulates primary productivity in many ecosystems.

Microorganisms help regulate nitrogen; however, wildlife such as birds, herbivores, and carnivores all play an important role in biogeochemical cycles and other critical ecosystem functions. Detritus from birds and mammals affects the availability of N for plants (NH_4+, NO_3) and soil nitrification rates. Wildlife helps to stabilize the amount of nitrogen (via ammonium and nitrate) in the forest system, allowing some to be taken up by plants and some to be used by microorganisms in the soil (Villar et al., 2020).

A recent study published in the journal Functional Ecology shows us how wildlife is needed to significantly enhance forest nutrient levels (Villar et al., 2020). "Animals, like the species in this study, evolved into a fine-scale way of positioning nutrients at the right concentrations, in the right places, at the right times, that enabled tropical rainforests to become among the richest ecosystems on the planet." Wildlife can transfer and amplify greater concentrations of forest soil nutrients.

The loss of wildlife directly impacts forest soil health. One likely direct cause of a decline in forest health is the rapid die-off of wildlife, including over 30 percent of our bird species. With the droppings (guano) and other benefits that birds bring (and other wildlife species in decline), forest soils are gaining a key source of natural fertilizer.

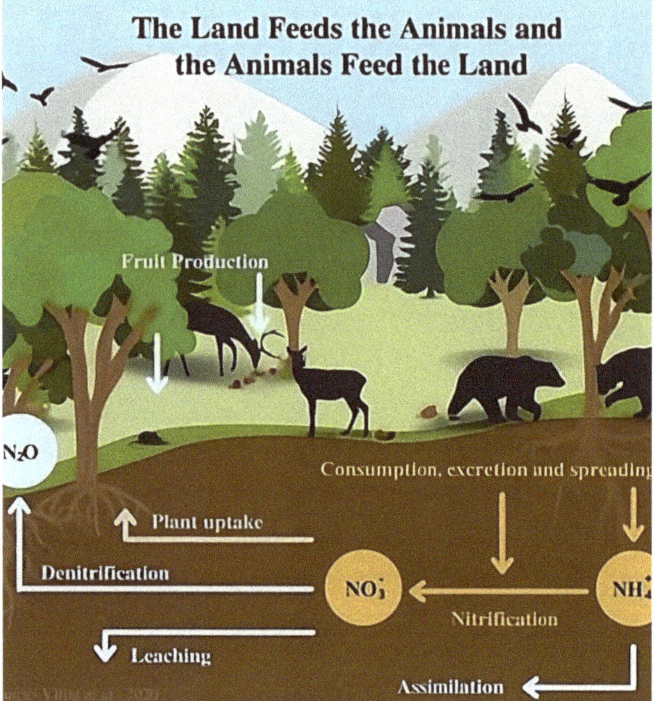

and most terrestrial arthropods, such as insects, are uricotelic organisms that convert toxic ammonia to uric acid or the closely related compound guanine (guano) rather than urea. In contrast, mammals (including humans) produce urea from ammonia (Molnar & Gair, 2015). Bird "manure" contains twice as much nitrogen and phosphorus as horse or cow manure (Jędrczak et al., 2014).

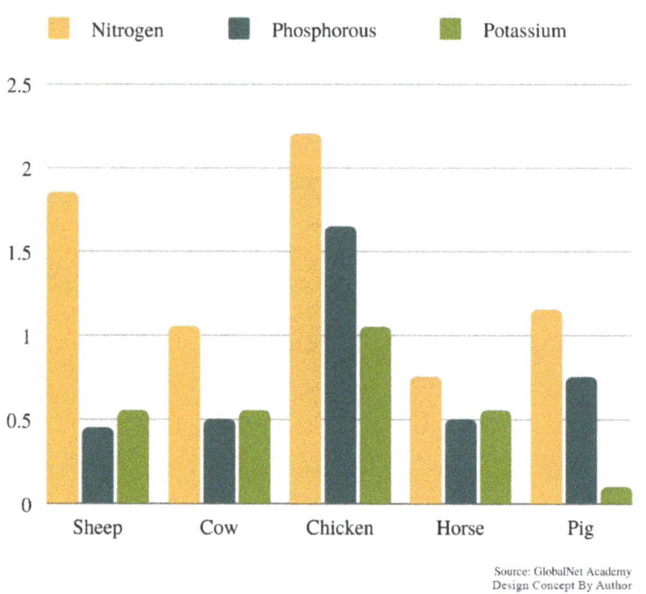

Loss of wildlife populations directly affects the amount of wildlife manure deposited on forest lands. While little research has been applied to gather specific soil data from animal manures on forest soil nutrients, species decline is well documented, and native trees have markedly improved in health when provided with organic nutrients such as chicken manure. Thus, the importance of animal biodiversity is a crucial component of healthy, functioning forest ecosystems, but it is neglected.

A growing body of scientific evidence in other parts of the world shows how forest animals are essential to natural, healthy forests. They perform pollination, seed dispersal, herbivory, and crucial roles affecting natural regeneration, soil quality, and even carbon storage (Bello et al., 2015).

While all wildlife is critical for the stability of soil integrity and forest health, birds play an essential role in enriching forest soil with their droppings. Birds, reptiles,

A significant benefit of bird "manure" is that it feeds soil microbes, allowing organic nutrients to break down faster and be available more quickly for plants. Bird guano is a complete fertilizer, as it contains high levels of macro-nutrients such as nitrogen, phosphorus, and potassium and essential micronutrients such as calcium needed for healthy plant growth.

Bird guano is also an excellent soil amendment as it adds organic matter to the soil, which improves moisture retention, soil structure, aeration, and drainage capability. Soil high in organic matter is less erosion-prone (Saliga III & Skelly, 2013).

However, that key source for soil health is now disappearing. Forty-eight percent of the world's bird species are in severe decline (Lees, 2022), and three billion birds have died across the United States and Canada during the last 50 years (Rosenberg et al., 2019).

Changing environmental conditions, habitat loss, resource scarcity, and forest degradation have contributed to the mass die-off of global avian populations (National Audubon Society, 2014). The effect of their disappearance on forests is simple: fewer nutrients reach forest soils and trees. This contributes to declining forest health along with drier soil conditions.

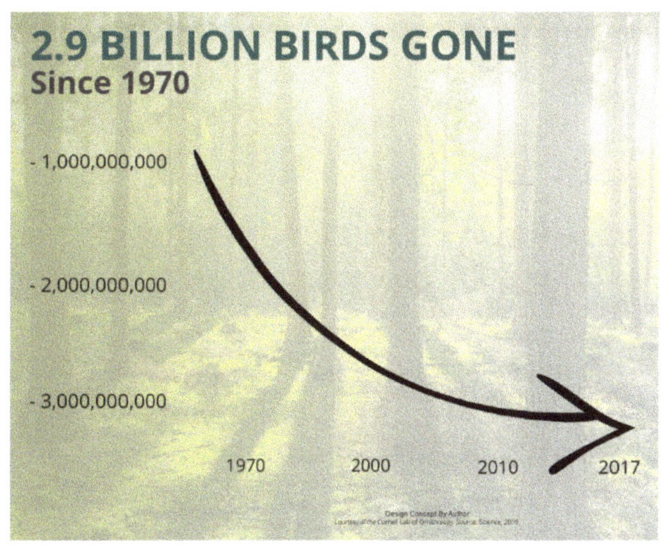

Forest Management Activity: Not In the Spring

Active forest management practices, such as cutting and thinning forest lands, can reduce biodiversity, especially when logging occurs in the spring. The reproductive success of many species is essential in maintaining biodiversity. Deforestation is one of the leading causes of extinction. But spring cutting is even more problematic because it lowers the chances of the next generation's survival, directly threatening a species' long-term survival.

Most birds and mammals rear their young in the spring. Many small animals' mate in spring, including birds and chipmunks, with short gestation or incubation periods. Larger animals with extended gestation periods, such as deer, mate during the fall and give birth during the spring. Logging, thinning, and prescribed burning can impact wildlife populations.

Cutting trees during breeding season raises severe problems because it removes food sources, shelter, and nesting sites wildlife rely on when rearing their young. It disrupts ecosystems and food chains from the ground up. Logging also increases predation risks and competition for food and shelter. Not only will birds and mammals have difficulty sustaining themselves, but they will also struggle to raise their young. Decreased resources and displacement during cutting, in combination with increased danger and competition, significantly lower the chances of survival of wildlife and their offspring.

Curbing spring cutting will protect wildlife and tree species when they are most vulnerable and prevent further loss of wildlife. Protecting species will mitigate exponential extinction rates. Any major forest management activity from mid-February to July 30th needs to be stringently reviewed for impact on wildlife and significantly reduced - with recommendations, when possible, to move the majority of "significant" forest management activities later in the year.

Forest management plans should include data about wildlife biodiversity, soil health, and nutrient levels and seek to maintain and attract wildlife. Preventing spring cutting protects biodiversity.

A Growing Problem: Human-Ignited Fires

Over 90 percent of wild-land fires in the United States are caused by people, according to the U.S. Department of Interior and the Insurance Information Institute (2021). Debris burning is the primary culprit in human-caused fires, at 29 percent, with arson the cause of 21 percent of fires. Equipment use causes 11 percent of fires; campfires and children playing with fireworks or matches each cause 5 percent. The Fourth of July is the biggest day for wildfires, with 7,762 fires ignited over the 21-year study period. (Balch et al., 2017).

Man-made fires have tripled the length of the average fire season in just the last 20 years from 46 days to 154 days! In addition, human-ignited fires tend to result in more extreme fire behavior and ecosystem impacts (Balch et al., 2017).

Balch et al. (2017) evaluated over 1.5 million government records of wildfires managed by state or federal agencies from 1992 to 2012. Theirs is the most comprehensive assessment of the role of human-started wildfires across the United States over the past two decades. The study documented "the pronounced expansion of wildfire extent, seasonality of wildfires, and increasing numbers of large wildfires through time as a result of human-related ignitions across the United States." This study revealed that in addition to expanding the number of fires, human-initiated fires raised the total area burned.

Fires Ignited by Humans

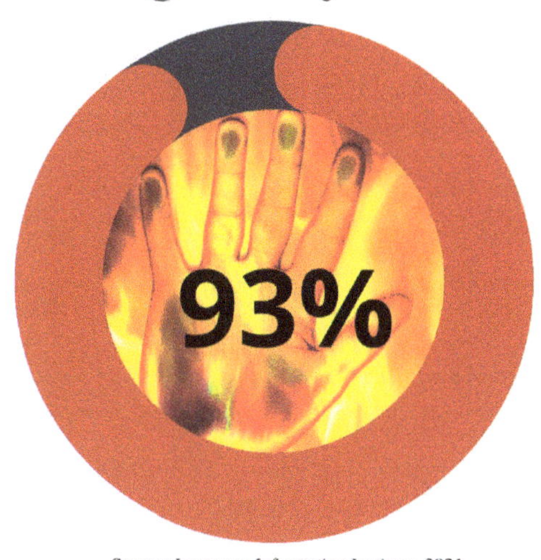

Source: Insurance Information Institute, 2021
Design Concept By Author

Number of wildfires and total burned area in California
(1992 to 2012)

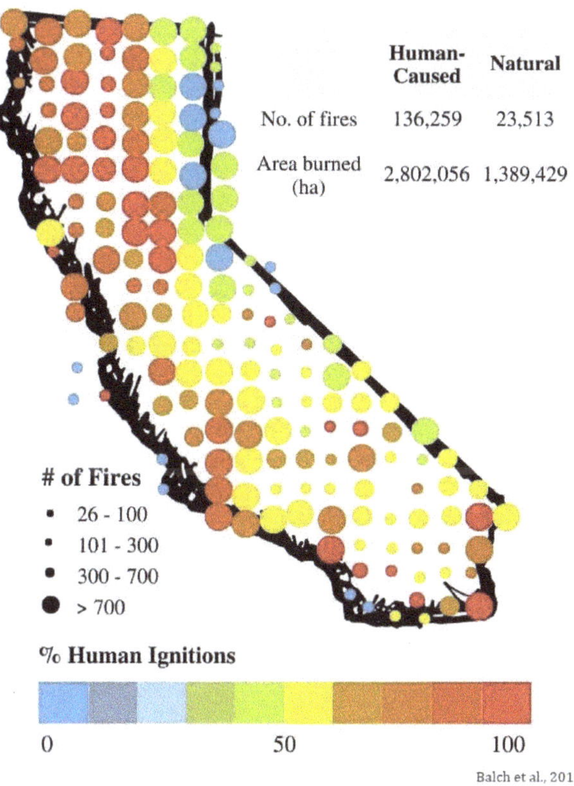

	Human-Caused	Natural
No. of fires	136,259	23,513
Area burned (ha)	2,802,056	1,389,429

Balch et al., 2017
Design Concept By Author

Human-sparked fires tend to burn faster and are more destructive. A study conducted by the University of California, Irvine, compiled daily high-resolution satellite data for 214 wildfires that burned in California between 2012 and 2018 (Hantson et al., 2022). The study found that human-sparked fires typically spread about 1.83 kilometers per day, more than twice as fast as the 0.83 kilometers per day for lightning-induced burns.

According to one of the study's authors, human-ignited fires also burned more intensely and killed double or triple the trees as slower-moving, lightning-caused ones (Hanston, 2020, as cited in Joosse, 2020). The researcher continues, "'These human-caused fires disproportionately impact the ecosystem…And though the ecosystem is fire-adapted, it's not adapted for 80 percent of trees to die, like we're seeing with some of these intense fires.'"

It now costs over $2 billion annually to fight fires nationwide. That figure does not include the impacts on recreational lands or the local economic impact that fires can have (U.S. Department of Interior, 2020). Ignitions caused by human activities substantially drive overall fire risk to ecosystems and economies. Actions to raise awareness and increase management in regions prone to human-started wildfires should be a focus of U.S. and California policy to reduce fire risk and associated hazards.

Although human influence has been proven to be a significant cause of fire ignition, nationally and statewide, this fact is little understood. Instead, the narrative that forests have been poorly managed - leading to increasing fires, has been widely promoted.

State policies can strongly influence public behavior. For example, California has strict littering laws with a $1,000 fine and up to one year of imprisonment if littering creates a substantial risk of injury or property damage. Signage indicating this is found throughout the state.

Yet there are few signs with warnings about igniting fires. In addition, fines do not reflect the enormous damage and loss of life from negligently starting a fire.

Source: Hanston, 2020
Design Concept By Author

Arrests are made in only about 10 percent of arson fires in the U.S. Even fewer cases are brought to court, indicating that greater enforcement and stricter penalties are needed (Pugmire et al., 2003). This reflects practices that are applied in many states and countries. New policies and practices must be implemented to reduce human-induced fires.

Public education, stricter guidance on burning, and increased fines need to be mandated to address the damage caused by anthropogenic wildfires actively. Public education programs and policy directives could target human behavior in ways that lessen trends in growing human-caused fires and wildfire risk. Public education campaigns are needed to alert the public about which activities to avoid and penalties for non-compliance. Since debris burning is a significant cause of fires, permitting this activity, requiring mandatory safety classes and routine on-site inspections, is recommended.

Forest Professionals & Policy Makers Must Address Ecological Realities Not Just Economic Factors

Many forestry managers worldwide continue to apply an outdated perspective and methodology that ignores scientific facts and critical environmental conditions in educating new forest managers. Too many professional foresters & policymakers focus on trees and forests from a purely economic perspective.

This attitude is understandable, given that forest industry representatives make money from cutting trees and selling board feet of timber. In California alone, timber harvests and wood product sales are a 39-billion-dollar industry! However, with climate change, species loss, and fires looming large, we can no longer do "business as usual" regarding forest management.

Today, training and educating forest managers must make a 360-degree change from present practices and focus. Professional foresters must assess Present Conditions Affecting Forest Health and Weigh the Ecological Values Trees Provide. Using California as an example, to become a registered forester, individuals must have seven years of forestry experience with time training under the tutelage of an existing certified forester and apply to the Board of Forestry. Once the field requirements are met, applicants must take and pass a written exam through the Professional Foresters Examining Committee (PFEC). To be issued a Registered Professional Forester license, they must get at least 75 percent of the exam correct and submit a licensing fee.

The California Board of Forestry and Fire Protection offers applicants study materials that emphasize facts for the timber industry's benefit versus scientifically sound information about the present state forests and factors contributing to their decline. Largely, absent also is information about forests' crucial values, such as biodiversity, atmospheric moisture, and carbon sequestration.

Among four books recommended for study by the Board, one is solely about commercial logging regulations, and another, a 1976 California Forestry Handbook, prioritizes informing applicants about the timber industry over forest health. The Handbook allocates more than 22 percent of its volume to direct logging industry topics, 11 times as much as the meager five pages (2 percent) dedicated to wildlife and ecology. While it describes "the tree" as a food, shelter, beauty, inspiration, and wood products provider,

---

[2] You can view the exam here: https://bof.fire.ca.gov/media/ebvc5h4x/april-2022-rpf-exam_ada.pdf

it ignores its function as a rainmaker, carbon sequesterer, and oxygen producer, among other beneficial roles. A third book about the California Forest Practice Program never addresses the importance of biodiversity and trees for the local and global environment, holistic land management practices, or soil nutrition, and the last recommended book is about roads.

Within a list of 20 exam study materials provided by the agency, eight are about fires, two are about commercial logging, and zero revolve around wildlife or the environment. The Registered Forester Exam fails to test essential knowledge about ecology and holistic land management. For example, in a recent exam, administered in April 2022, about 60 percent of the questions revolved around fires, while forest ecology comprised less than five percent of the exam.

Applicants were not tested on their understanding of the environmental impacts of thinning trees, for example, which releases significant amounts of carbon while losing all of the many environmental values the trees used to provide. Failing to include questions about climate change, wildlife, drought, and forest values allows applicants to receive their license without having a thorough understanding of these topics.

Furthermore, the exam content employs biased diction that implies outdated understandings of forestry concepts. Trees are referred to as "fuel," which leads test-takers to regard trees only as food for fires and not as providing

enormous ecological values such as carbon sinks, oxygen producers, habitat for wildlife, and water cycle regulators. The exam phrases specific questions, such as "What types of wildlife commonly benefit from wildland fire?" and "What is Beneficial Fire?" but fails to test applicants on their knowledge of the detrimental impacts of things like excessive fires and drought, excess carbon in the atmosphere, and global rising temperatures. Nor are applicants informed of the devastating impacts and regularity of human-ignited fires.

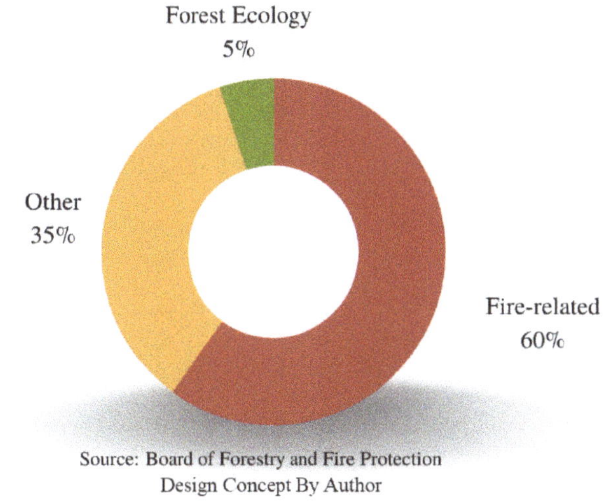

Source: Board of Forestry and Fire Protection
Design Concept By Author

Professionals in forest management must understand the impacts of drought, atmospheric weather conditions, and UV radiation, as well as the importance of biodiversity needs and soil values. Forest agencies and certified registered foresters should consider trees as more than "fuel" and wood products and understand trees' many values, such as carbon sequestration, oxygen production, habitat creation, shade, cooling, and flood minimization. Forester training and certification programs should equip future foresters with up-to-date scientific knowledge of the systems they will manage. California-certified foresters should know how to assess wind conditions, soil health, and wildlife values and understand the impacts of changing weather patterns, extreme heat, drought, and increased UV radiation.

Protecting ecosystems and biodiversity should not be balanced against other objectives and values as if they were equally important. Protecting and restoring forest lands should be the goal of balancing environmental, social, and economic objectives in forest management. This is because a healthy biodiverse ecosystem is the very foundation upon which All other needs depend.

Forest Management & Policies Must Reference New Scientific Data

As the world's climate warms, new technology is helping to assess earth systems and responses to present conditions. Yet, policy decisions ignore the newest scientific data and fail to apply new factors influencing forest health. For example, professional foresters rarely consider soil quality, UV radiation, wildlife biodiversity, and other factors when making forest management suggestions. Yet, knowledge of these conditions is essential to make meaningful determinations.

Laser-Guided Spectroscopy

One innovative method is laser-guided spectroscopy, which reads the light reflected from trees to measure their water content and other key health indicators. With these methods, the Carnegie Airborne Observatory can read 8 million trees per hour. It is one of the world's most advanced Earth mapping and data analytics platforms.

Forests seen without a spectrometer.

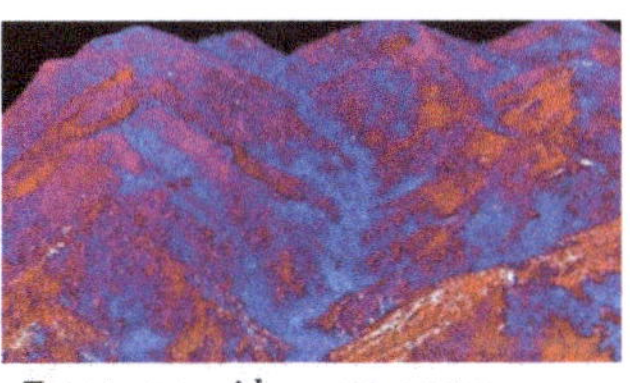

Forests seen with a spectrometer.
Extreme lack of moisture

The observatory measures three important chemical properties: the amount of water and sugar in the tree and the nitrogen in the tree canopy. This matters because even green and healthy trees may be drought-stressed beyond their limits and dead within the next 6-12 months.

For example, the observatory found that millions of trees in California showed dangerously low amounts of internal water—even though they look green to the naked eye (Asner et al., 2015)!

The observatory is presently working on a worldwide forest study. Focusing on forests in the Southern Hemisphere, in tropical parts of Asia, and Central America, the team combines laser-based measurements of forest height from NASA's ICESat mission with other remote sensing data, as well as with information from more than 4,000 ground-level inventories of tree height and biomass. They can map forest structure and carbon density down to a resolution of 1 kilometer. The 2.5-billion-hectare study area holds a total of 247 gigatonnes of carbon, the team estimates (Saatchi et al., 2011).

Vegetation Drought Response Index (VegDRI)

In addition to the Carnegie Observatory, two commonly used satellite-based drought indicators are the Vegetation Health Index (VHI) and Vegetation Drought Response Index (VegDRI). VHI is a National Oceanic and Atmospheric Administration satellite that monitors the health of vegetation, regardless of the cause. Poor vegetation health, as indicated by the VHI, may be due to stress caused by drought, stress caused by too much water (e.g., flooding), or some other cause (such as insect infestation). The VegDRI, on the other hand, is monitored by the National Drought Mitigation Center (NDMC) in collaboration with several other partners. It is a national map covering the contiguous U.S. and provides regional to sub-county scale information about drought's effects on vegetation.

Both satellites provide valuable in situ observations that provide crucial data to support weather forecasters, industries and economies, and government and private sector leaders. The trouble is the implications of the data from Laser-Guided Spectroscopy, VHI, and VegDRI—that forests are critical for storing carbon and healing the atmosphere and that trees are stressed by changing climatic conditions—are rarely considered in forest management determinations. Professional foresters and federal and state agencies ignore this data, and wildfires are incorrectly blamed on a lack of forest management instead of drought, dry soils, and dry trees.

Both satellites provide valuable in situ observations that provide crucial data to support weather forecasters, industries and economies, and government and private sector leaders. The trouble is the implications of the data from Laser-Guided Spectroscopy, VHI, and VegDRI—that forests are critical

for storing carbon and healing the atmosphere and that trees are stressed by changing climatic conditions—are rarely considered in forest management determinations. Professional foresters

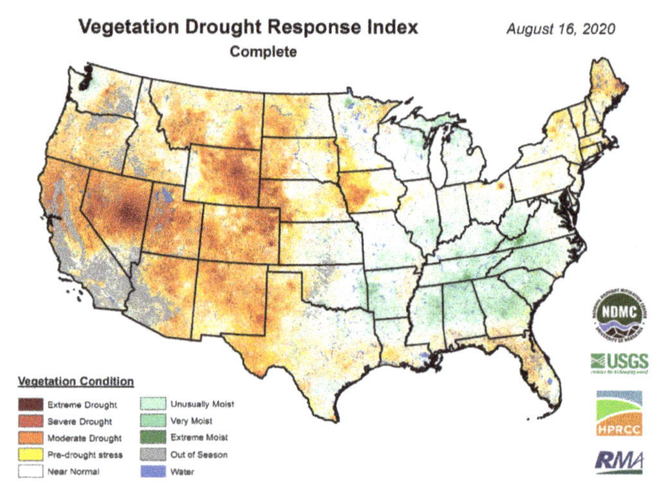

VegDRI revealed severe to moderate drought conditions across California and the West on the day of the August Complex Fire.

Fires Are No Longer "Normal" Due to 50-Year Increase in Global Temperatures

Since 1880, the average global temperature has increased by 1.9 degrees Fahrenheit (NASA, 2022). California's average summer temperatures have risen a whopping 3 degrees Fahrenheit, with more than half of that increase in the past 50 years (Scripps Institution of Oceanography, n.d.). This has produced a new normal of fires with unprecedented severity, speed, and spread.

According to a study in Proceedings of the National Academy of Sciences, since 1984, heightened temperatures in the Western United States have caused fires to spread across an additional 16,000 square miles than they otherwise would have—an area larger than the states of Massachusetts and Connecticut combined (Abatzoglou and Williams, 2016). In addition, fire radiative power (FRP), the rate of radiant heat emitted by a fire, is becoming more intense. California and Oregon's 2020 fire seasons had the highest fire intensity of the past 18 years (Borunda, 2020).

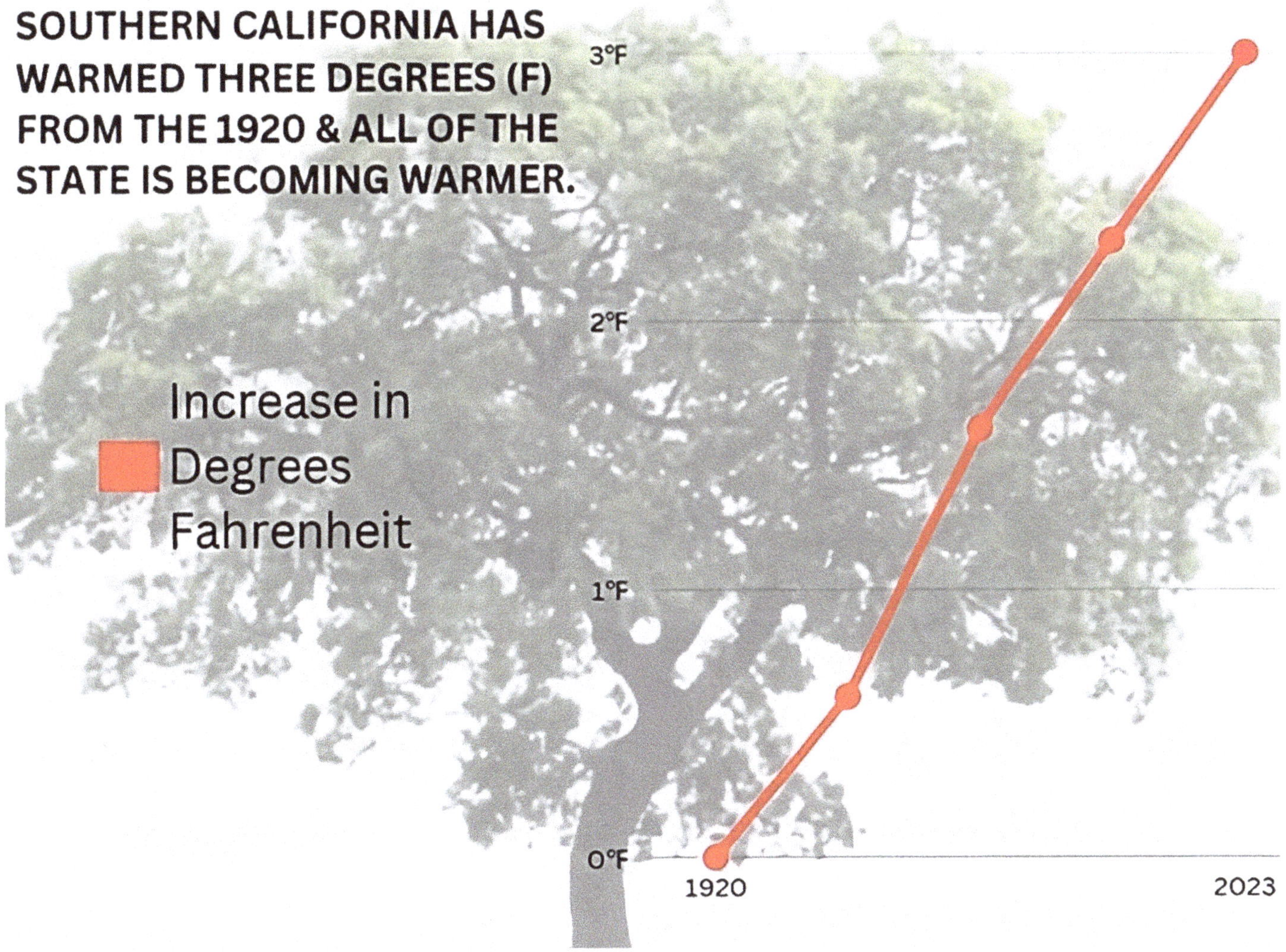

Woods Hole Oceanographic Institution found that California's 2012-2014 drought was the worst in 1,200 years (Griffin & Anchukaitis, 2014). And while the state had seen similar precipitation levels, what was unprecedented was the level of heat in the atmosphere—a consequence of climate change.

Arid conditions create a tinderbox, for wildfires can ignite from actions as simple as sparks flying from a trailer dragging on the road or a faulty power line. Hence, today's mega-fires (Abatzoglou and Williams, 2016).

Today's fires are more plentiful, hotter, faster, and more destructive than ever. Some recent fires have even earned a new name: "firenados." With flames reaching 45,000 feet, these tall, pyro-cumulus clouds ravage landscapes and communities with lightning, thunder, and high winds (Arthur, 2020). Firenados are a powerful marker of the unprecedented speed and severity of largely human-caused fires. In 2020 alone, California's wildfires burned 4.2 million acres, damaged or destroyed 10,500 structures, and killed 31 people (Insurance Information Institute, 2021).

Unlike fires of the past that allowed burned habitats to recover, the roasting fires change the region's biodiversity and keep some native plant species from propagating by turning their seeds and acorns into nothing more than ash and smoke. These fires are nothing short of "apocalyptic." Although numerous factors drive recent increases in fire activity, warming and drying have significantly raised fire-season fuel aridity. Anthropogenic climate change will continue to heat the earth and worsen Western U.S. fire activity in the decades to come. Add to this the fact that humans ignite the vast majority of fires today and are more deadly, and we arrive at the present untenable situation.

With this in mind, we must stop fires before they start. Once begun, today's fires may turn into unstoppable firenado's, leaving mass destruction in their wake.

Increased UV Radiation Is Damaging Forests:
Thinning Makes Them More Susceptible

On Dec. 29, 2003, a world-record UV index 43.3 was detected at Bolivia's Licancabur volcano (Cabrol et al., 2014). The UV index forecasts the strength of the sun's ultraviolet rays. The observatory's instruments recorded the highest UV radiation ever recorded on Earth. The UV index of 43 is more similar to surface radiation on Mars than typical conditions on Earth, and the reading is well above the mid-20s routinely measured in the high Andes.

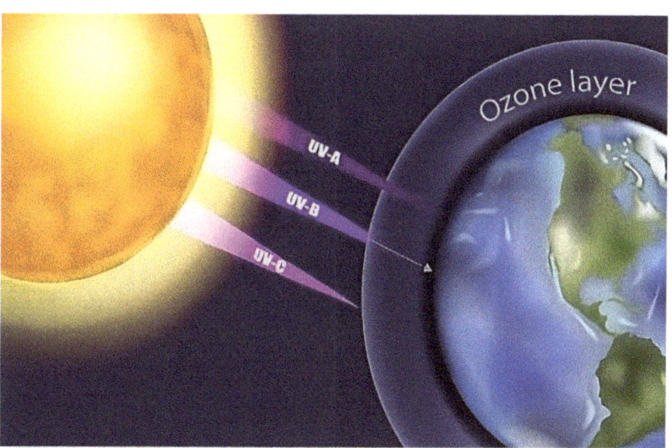

The stratosphere is the most crucial layer of Earth's atmosphere in protecting the planet from excessive UV radiation. The stratosphere's ozone layer typically absorbs 97-99 percent of incoming UV-B radiation, which is crucial to ensuring Earth's life is protected from harmful concentrations of UV-B radiation (Ritchie and Roser, 2018). The emission of ozone-depleting substances (ODS),

(CFCs), hydrochlorofluorocarbons (HCFCs), methyl chloride and bromide, and halons increased rapidly until the 1980s. These releases led to a "hole" in the ozone layer.

The ozone hole was first discovered in the 1960s, and the Montreal Protocol was enacted to ensure that the world's nations limit the production and consumption of ozone-depleting substances.

(ODS) into the atmosphere (UN Environment Programme, 2016). It was hoped that the ozone hole would begin to return to normal in 40-50 years, yet the ozone hole has not fully healed. Recent ozone holes, years after the

It takes decades to cleanse CFCs and ozone-depleting substances from the atmosphere, and concentrations peaked around 1994 (World Meteorological.

Organization, 1998). Today, we

---

[3] Well before the expected stratospheric ozone layer recovery date of 2050, ozone's effects on climate may become the main driver of ozone loss in the stratosphere. As a result, ozone recovery may not be complete until 2060 or 2070. (See Strahan and Douglass, 2018).

Importantly, CFCs and halogens are greenhouse gases with a high capacity to trap heat in the Earth's atmosphere up to 10,000 times higher than carbon dioxide! Sources estimate that the climate benefits of the Montreal Protocol to stop these gases can be five to six times that of the Kyoto Protocol (Velders et al., 2012).

NASA released details of the size and duration of last year's Antarctic ozone hole. The NASA Aura satellite measured the Antarctic ozone hole as 24.8 million square kilometers at its largest between September and October 2021 (NASA Earth Observatory, 2021). It was the longest-lasting and one of the largest and deepest holes since the ozone layer monitoring began 40 years ago. (The September 2020 ozone hole was also one of the most significant ozone holes ever recorded.) (NASA). As a result, NASA scientists analyzing 30 years of satellite data have found that the amount of ultraviolet (UV) radiation reaching Earth's surface has increased markedly (Voiland, 2010).

The New Arctic Ozone Hole

In addition, and quite surprisingly, while it was the Antarctica ozone hole that has concerned scientists since the 1960s, starting in 2011, scientists noticed a startling change: a new ozone hole in Earth's atmosphere in addition to the Antarctic ozone hole, this time in the Northern Hemisphere.

The new Arctic ozone hole was the largest recorded in 2020, expanding over an area roughly three times the size of Greenland (Specktor, 2020). This hole was significantly more significant than the ozone hole first seen over the Arctic in 2011, which destroyed over 80 percent of the ozone between 18 and 20 kilometers altitude by the end of that winter (Lindsey, 2012).

Now that Earth's poles are experiencing this phenomenon, scientists and climate advocates are sounding the alarm. The Arctic tends to have more variable temperatures than its Southern counterpart, but in 2020, powerful winds trapped cold air in a "polar vortex," creating conditions suitable for ozone depletion.

(Specktor, 2020). Scientists believe that the "polar vortex" in 2020 can be traced back to record-high sea surface temperatures in the North Pacific, a symptom of global warming.

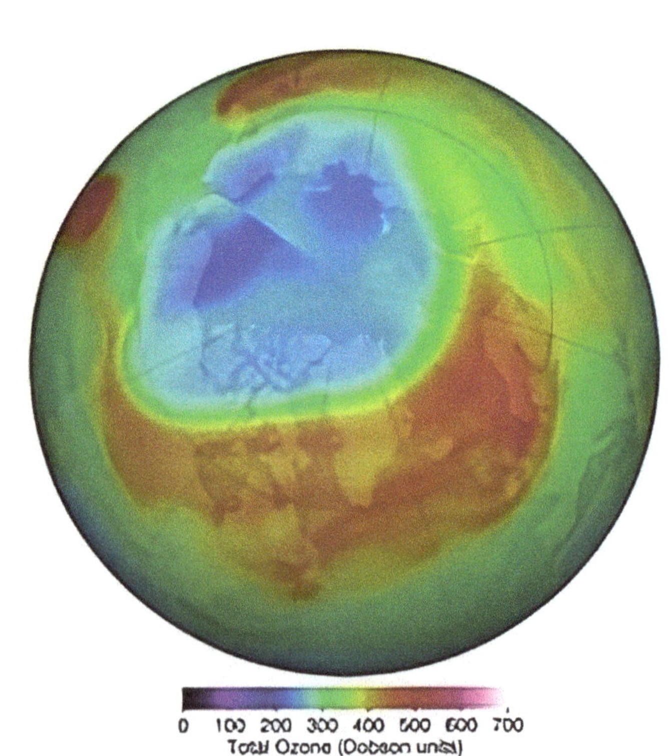

The thinning of stratospheric ozone in the Arctic has been connected to weather anomalies and higher rates of UV damage across the entire Northern Hemisphere (Zurich, 2022). Scientists warn that "severe Arctic ozone loss could form again, as long as certain dynamic conditions are satisfied," conditions climate change creates

UV B & C Radiation Can Be Harmful to Planetary Life

Excessive solar UV radiation compromises the health of humans in terrestrial and aquatic ecosystems. Short-wavelength UV-B radiation damages DNA diminishes photosynthesis, and decreases viability in eggs and larval stages of terrestrial and aquatic animals (Hader et al., 2011). Ultraviolet radiation is the primary etiologic agent in developing skin cancers in humans. Deadly skin cancers have doubled over the last three decades (Centers for Disease Control and Prevention, 2015).

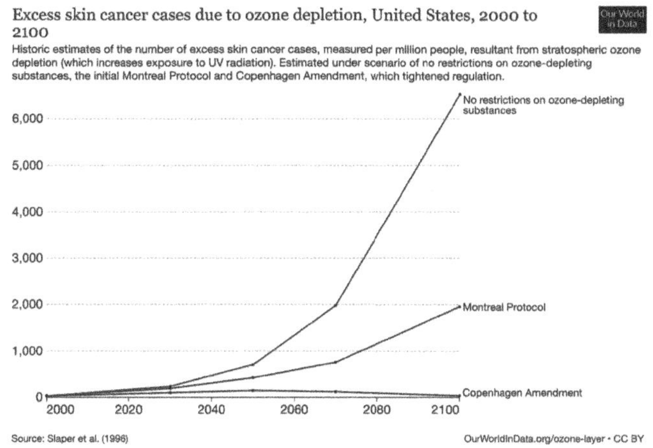

Plants are not immune from UV damage. Trees and forests cannot avoid exposure to enhanced levels of UV-B radiation and are especially at risk. UV-B can sterilize and burn foliage in high enough concentrations, impairing metabolic processes such as photosynthesis and carbon sequestration (Climate Policy Watcher, 2022).

Studies have indicated that "Increased UV-B radiation on the earth's surface due to depletion of the stratospheric ozone layer is one of the changes of current climate-change pattern. The harmful effects of UV-B radiation on photosynthesis and photosynthetic productivity of plants are reviewed. A perusal of relevant literature reveals that UV-B radiation damages the photosynthetic apparatus of green plants at multiple sites. The damage sites include an oxygen-evolving complex, D1/D2 reaction center proteins, and other components on the donor and acceptor sides of PS II. The radiation inactivates light-harvesting complex II and alters gene expression for synthesizing PS II reaction center proteins" (Kataria et al., 2014).

With the effects of more significant radiation underway, already weakened forests could experience greater damage from pests and herbivory and the increasingly common extreme weather events. Reproduction could be further limited, impairing our forests' productivity in the long run. Trees that are damaged and incapable of reproducing, resulting in a decrease in forest growth, carbon sequestration, and overall productivity

"Malformations in fossilized gymnosperm pollen from the extinction interval during the end-Permian

shield deterioration." (Benca et al., 2018) Scientists tested by observing the effects of UV-B regimes on pollen development and reproductive success in living conifers (Benca et al., 2018). They found that pollen malformation frequencies increase fivefold under high UV-B intensities. All trees survived but were sterilized under enhanced UV-B.

They concluded that heightened UV-B stress could have contributed to pollen malformation production and deforestation during Permian-Triassic crisis intervals. "By reducing the fertility of several widespread gymnosperm lineages, pulsed ozone shield weakening could have induced repeated terrestrial biosphere destabilization and food web collapse without exerting a direct "kill" mechanism on land plants or animals. These findings challenge the paradigm that mass extinctions require kill mechanisms and suggest that modern conifer forests may be considerably more vulnerable to anthropogenic ozone layer depletion than expected" (Benca et al., 2018).

While stopping harmful releases of CFCs and other chemicals that cause UV radiation is critical to protecting trees and all life on Earth, in the interim, maintaining and creating greater tree and canopy density is one way to help protect plants and people locally and regionally.

Older, mature trees in undisturbed forests and large groves offer each other shade by restricting the amount of UV B reaching each individual. For example, UVB radiation was reduced to 1-2% of its original radiance under dense trees that provide a shaded canopy.

However, in disturbed (logged) forests where trees were thinned, UV B radiation was at 17 percent, with an even more significant increase during the leafless season at 30 percent (Brown et al., 1994). In a Swedish study, birch forests limited 26.4 percent of UV-B (Fraser et al., 2011).

Plants have some limited means to adapt and protect themselves from slightly raised levels of UV-B radiation. Over half a billion tons of isoprene are emitted annually from trees worldwide (Cotton, 2015). This chemical is a "sunscreen" to shield plants from mild UV radiation. In addition, a chemical found in the leaves of trees and plants, sinapoyl malate, has been found to absorb UV radiation without harming the plant (Dean et al., 2014).

However, these protection strategies are limited against excessive UV B radiation, and the most significant protection comes from higher numbers of trees in a forest or a grove. In areas of greater canopy density, more leaves if trees are solitary or in thinned forests where more UV-B can reach them. In this case, there is more excellent protection in numbers.

While a relatively obscure subject in forestry, the benefits of canopy density on ultraviolet radiation have been well studied to mitigate rising urban temperatures and ill effects on residents. For example, studies conducted in cities of varying latitudes across the globe overwhelmingly indicate that tree cover density directly correlates to the amount of UV radiation pedestrians receive. In Seoul, South Korea, cemeteries and parklands had the most significant measure of UV defense compared to land with less tree cover, such as property zoned for commercial use and transportation (Ryeol Na et al., 2014).

A solution to protecting trees from increased UV-B radiation is relatively simple: maintain trees and Forest density, thus mitigating the amount of UV radiation each tree receives. This tactic will not completely resolve the problem of UV damage, but it is clear that lone trees and thinned forests are far more susceptible to UV radiation.

Logging Releases the Highest Amount of Carbon

Wildlands store 25 percent of global anthropogenic emissions (UC Davis, 2021). The thinning of California's forests will release a dramatic amount of carbon into the atmosphere while removing a critical carbon sink, accelerating climate change. Logging proponents often claim that thinning

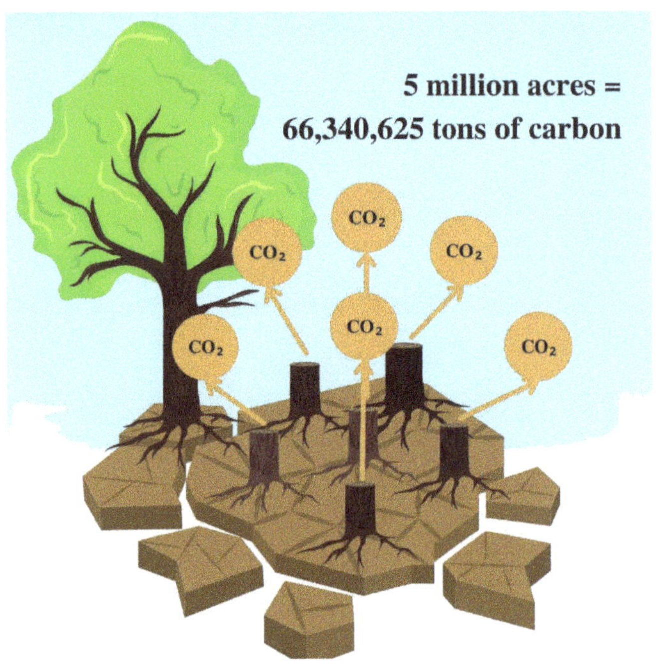

percent of the carbon in logged trees and forest lands quickly becomes greenhouse gas emissions, and when trees are cut down and burned to generate "biomass" electricity, 100 percent of the carbon is emitted (Smith et al., 2019). Incinerating wood for energy emits even more carbon than coal (Sterman et al., 2018).

On average, an acre of California forestland contains 2,875 cubic feet of wood volume. Each cubic foot can store roughly 14.20 pounds (.0071 tons) of carbon (Christensen et al., 2008 & Mader, 2007). That means that an average un-thinned acre stores a total of 20.41 tons of sequestered carbon (Mader, 2007 & United States Forest Service, 2016). Assuming that our forestry agencies cut 65% of each

leads to the survival of more trees in thinned plots, thus storing carbon, yet logging releases anywhere from five to ten times the carbon as wildfire, bark beetles, and drought combined (Harris et al., 2016).
Approximately 28 percent of a tree's carbon is emitted from branches when they are burned after logging operations (Campbell et al., 2007). An additional 53 percent of the carbon is emitted as "waste" in the manufacturing and

[4] We are still refining this calculation.

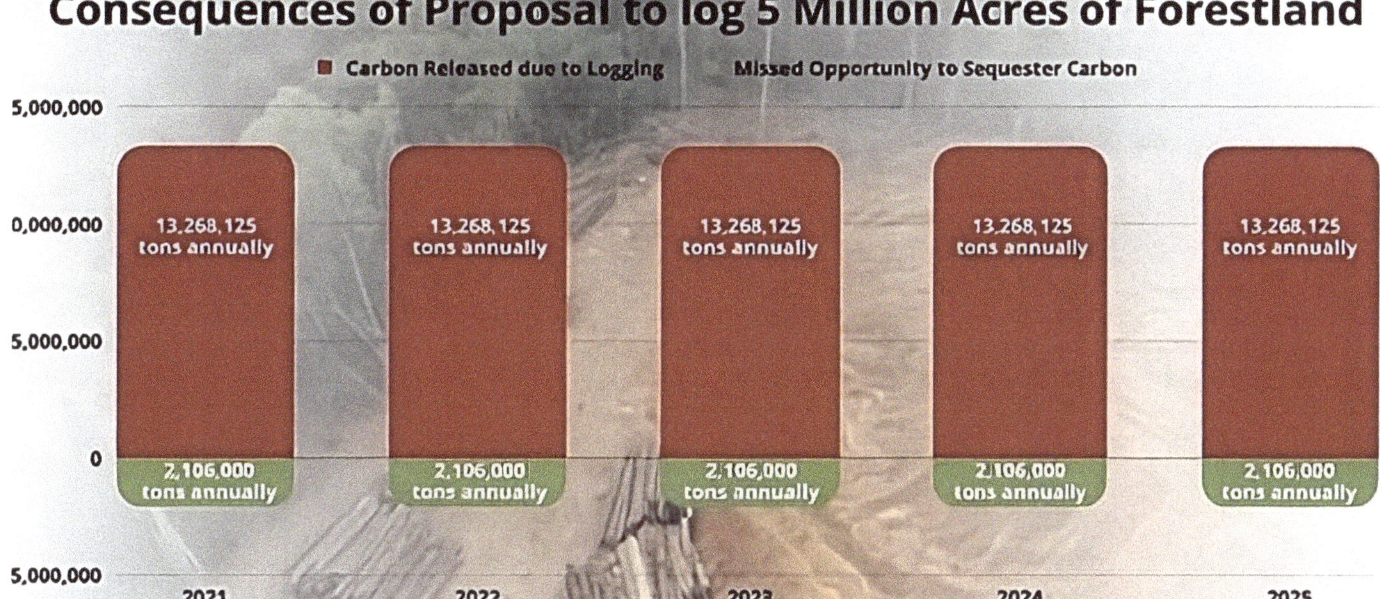

9,343,750,000 cubic feet of wood, releasing 66,340,625 tons of carbon.

This thinning measure of 5.07 tons of CO2 per year (EPA, 2022) amounts to putting 13,083,310 vehicles on the road! Additionally, an average acre of California forest currently sequesters an additional average of 3.24 tons of carbon per year (Mader, 2007). Logging 65% of 5 million acres will mean failing to sequester an additional 10,530,000 tons of carbon in only five years (2020-2025) [4]

It has been estimated that protecting U.S. and California public forestlands from logging would reduce direct carbon emissions and increase the annual drawdown of atmospheric CO2 by 84 million tons per year (Depro et al., 2008).

Protecting forest ecosystems is critical in limiting global warming and extreme weather events leading to flooding, desertification, heat, and droughts. Since wood harvest represents most carbon losses from U.S. forests, increasing the U.S. net forest carbon sink requires shifts in current forest management practices. Achieving a global, economy-wide balance between anthropogenic emissions and removals by carbon sinks will require both more emission reductions and more carbon sequestration from the forest sector.

Now that the United States has rejoined The Paris Agreement, California should seek to limit emissions and increase carbon sequestration. Under the Paris Agreement, the U.S. agreed to cut its emissions by up to 52 percent this decade compared to 2005(United Nations, 2015).

The agreement asserts that achieving global climate targets requires protecting and restoring forests (United Nations, 2015). However, the success of this new commitment depends on a unified approach that holds countries globally accountable for protecting their climate-critical forests. In particular, mature native trees are the most

Forest Thinning Can Increase Fire Speed and Temperature, Leading to Faster, Hotter Fires

Forest thinning seeks to reduce fire risk by removing trees ("fuel"). However, this practice is flawed. One of the most extensive studies has shown that thinned forests are subjected to more intensive fires than non-managed forest lands with greater tree density.

Investigators surveyed over ten years of data and 1,500 fires encompassing 9.5 million hectares of pine and mixed-conifer forests in the western United States. They determined that fires burned "more ferociously in thinned and heavily managed forest lands versus less severely in un-thinned forests, despite having
more biomass for fuel" (Bradley et al., 2016).   Bradley et al., 2016.

According to the authors: "We found no evidence to support the prevailing forest/fire management hypothesis that higher levels of forest protections are associated with more severe fires based on the RF and linear mixed-effects modeling approaches. On the contrary, using over three decades of fire severity data from relatively frequent-fire pine and mixed-conifer forests throughout the western United States, we found support for the opposite conclusion— burn severity tended to be higher in areas with lower levels of protection status (more intense management), after accounting for topographic and climatic conditions in all three model runs. Thus, we rejected the prevailing

forest management view that areas with higher protection levels burn most severely during wildfires."

An OPB and ProPublica analysis of September 2020 agreed with this hypothesis and found that, on average, recently clear-cut private lands burned hotter than biomass-stocked federal lands, while logged public lands burned at the same intensity as unlogged public lands (Schick & Burns, 2020). Another study found that even under "best case" scenarios, thinning damaged 3.4 to 6.0

The Creek and Douglas Complex fires exemplify the failures of thinning to reduce fire severity. In the 2020 Creek Fire that burned 153,738 acres across the Sierra National Forest and private forestlands, logging that had been carried out to minimize fire damage was associated with higher fire severity. Areas that underwent fuel-reduction logging endured the most severe brunt of the fire. In contrast, forests that experienced prescribed fire or wildfire but no thinning or logging experienced the least severe fire impacts (Hanson, 2021). During the 2013 Douglas Complex Fire in Oregon, private industrial timber plantations burned 30 percent more severely than federal forestlands (Schick & Burns, 2020).

Similarly, a study assessing California spotted owl habitats found areas logged for "fuel reduction" were subjected to higher fire severity, with the highest severity in areas with commercial logging (Hanson, 2021).

A key reason why thinned acres burn hotter and faster is because thinning helps air—and thus fires—move through forests. Fires need oxygen as much as they need fuel to burn. Thinned and logged forests have decreased density, allowing winds to travel uninterrupted and gather at greater speed (Western Watersheds Project, n.d.). Stronger winds provide more oxygen, so fires move rapidly and burn ferociously. High winds are a significant factor in the massive fires we see today.

Wildfires typically reach top speeds of six miles per hour in forests and 14 miles per hour in grasslands (Siegal,

2017). However, Northern California's Glass Fire traveled at 40 mph, burning about 67,500 acres and destroying 1,555 structures. Its speed was mainly due to high wind conditions (Sweeney, 2020 & Insurance Information Institute, 2021).

Natural, biodiverse, and non-managed forests tend to have dense plant life, making it harder for oxygen to travel through and feed fires. In addition, forests with high populations of plants tend to have more surrounding air moistur. This is because of evapotranspiration— the process where plants and trees produce atmospheric water vapor. The soil of a natural unmanaged forest will also likely contain more moisture due to shade cooling the ground, less UV radiation reaching the forest floor, and more wildlife. Moist forests impede the spread of fires.

Logging and thinning forest lands will not prevent forest fires and may cause fires to move more quickly and ferociously. To date, most regulations and funding have been applied to forest thinning. However, there is no proof that these measures will reduce fires.

The myth that modern fires are caused by a lack of "management" does not hold. Thus, forest managers and policymakers must rethink current forest and fire management decisions and avoid supporting plans that suspend forest protections or facilitate cutting in the name of fire safety.

Rather than slowing the spread of wildfires, thinning compromises forest defenses by removing the largest, most

To Save Lives & Protect Property: Property Owners Need Better Advice & Financial Support

Too often, landowners are advised to thin out trees on their more significant acreage and surrounding neighborhood and forest lands. While this may make sense for trees close to or overhanging built structures, many landowners waste precious time and resources cutting and removing trees further from their dwellings rather than fireproofing their buildings and planning an escape route.

This is a direct result of the significant involvement of forestry industry lobbyists in "advising" on fire protection steps and suggesting policies focused on tree cutting, which provides revenue for the industry. This results in insufficient attention to directly fireproofing buildings and having adequate emergency plans and exits.

Private landowners must understand that thinning surrounding acreage of forest lands will not stop a fire from coming onto their property, especially since most fires are started by lit embers that can travel up to a mile in extreme winds!
Landowners should be advised to realign their priorities towards installing fire-retardant siding material and water features, removing fallen dry leaves or sticks near their facilities, and working with neighbors to develop a well-organized evacuation plan. In addition, government subsidies could be established to help cover the costs and/or provide tax incentives for these measures.

Residents must be advised that fireproofing immediately around the building and the building itself is the best way to prevent damage. Governments could provide tax incentives and subsidies similar to those used for solar to assist landowners in upgrading their structures to be fire resilient.

Improve Communication Systems to Prevent Loss of Life

Preventing loss of human life is a priority in fire scenarios, and most people killed by fires have too little information or incorrect information. Improving communication systems statewide and at the community level to provide accurate and timely information about fire severity and movement and evacuation updates is vital.

There is an urgent need to improve fire communications systems to save lives. However, in state budgets, these needs take a back seat to fire prevention strategies focused on cutting and thinning forest lands. CALFIRE's proposed 2022-2024 budget appropriates $382 million for Wildfire Fuel Breaks, whereas Community Hardening only receives $44 million, with only $9 million going to Land Use Planning and Public Education (Petek, 2022).

Forest fire prevention projects, which primarily fund deforestation and thinning, receive over forty times (40) the funding of public education campaigns.

Since 2015, California wildfires have caused the deaths of nearly 200 people (Center for
Biological Diversity, 2021). Most can be attributed to failures in California's emergency communication infrastructure. Inadequate, uncoordinated, and understaffed losses in the state's communications apparatus have transcended county

lines and eroded the public's trust in the government to keep people safe from fires (Fitzsimons & Helsel, 2020) (Phillips, 2018) (Stidham et al., 2011).
For a population to safely retreat from a fire threat, they need to know its location, direction, speed of travel, and the best escape routes. Yet, this basic information is too often lacking, leading to more significant mortality than necessary.

For example, California's fire

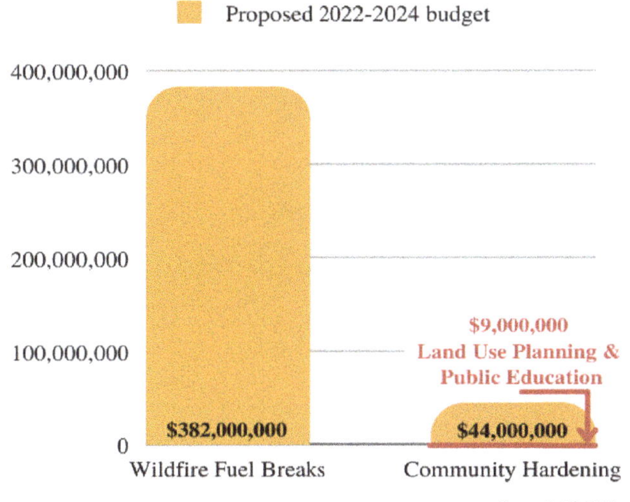

Headline		Date	Link
"Man, woman who died in California fires were ready to flee but stayed because of 'erroneous information'"	NBC	9/16/2020	https://www.nbcnews.com/news/us-news/man-woman-who-died-california-fires-were-ready-flee-stayed-n1240200
"Troubled evacuation in Paradise: How a malfunctioning alert system kept citizens in harm's way"	Gov1	10/30/2021	https://www.gov1.com/emergency-manageme nt/articles/troubled-evacuation-in-paradisehow-a-malfunctioning-alert-system-kept-citize ns-in-harms-way-RTkXZZAyUSmdj7kG/
"Failure to Communicate: Orange County Wildfires Highlight Long Standing Emergency Communication Problems"	Voice of	12/21/2020	https://voiceofoc.org/2020/12/failure-to-com municate-orange-county-wildfires-highlight-lo ng-standing-emergency-communication-problems/
"Californians say they didn't receive emergency wildfire alerts"	CNN	10/15/2017	https://www.cnn.com/2017/10/13/us/californi a-fires-emergency-alerts/index.html
"Many Residents Did Not Receive Emergency Alerts During The Camp Fire. Will You Be Warned If A Disaster Is Heading Your Way?"		7/11/2019	https://www.capradio.org/articles/2019/07/11 /emergency-alert-will-you-be-notified-if-a-wild fire-is-heading-toward-your-town/
"Camp Fire created a black hole of communication"	Chico	12/17/2018	https://www.chicoer.com/2018/12/17/camp-fi re-created-a-black-hole-of-communication/

With climate change increasing and the likelihood of continuing severe fires, greater Emphasis on state and local fire emergency and evacuation communication & information is needed to Protect Human Life.

Shifting funding away from ineffective, costly fire prevention strategies like cutting trees and building a robust, dependable communication system will save lives. This will require an overhaul and investment in improving fire response communication systems and protocols to provide timely emergency response and specific localized information - such as evacuation routes.

Anthropogenic Climate Change Is a Fact: But the Problem is Not Population Density!

Rising CO2 levels, UV radiation, and higher global temperatures are human-caused and creating havoc on the planet's ecological systems. These global maladies are some of the greatest threats facing humankind. Then why is nothing being done about them? Thirty years ago, during the 1990s, there was a more cohesive understanding of climate change and its impact on the planet.

Today, too many people, especially in America and other Western nations, believe that planetary global warming does not exist or is good for the planet. [xxiii] Unfortunately, as public awareness began to take hold, corporate owners in the oil and gas industries recognized that people were beginning to pinpoint those largely responsible. Exxon Mobile knew its industrial practices could lead to devastating climate change as early as 1977. According to "Inside Climate News" and Harvard University investigations, this was 11 years before global warming became a public issue. [5] Yet, instead of revealing this information that affects all life on the planet, the company not only refused to go public, but it did a deep dive into obfuscation of the truth.

The company spent thousands of dollars promoting climate change denial and misinformation. This was the same unethical approach used by the tobacco industry to lie about smoking's health risks to save their profits. This led to many more people developing cancer and dying from smoking. Today, company-led propaganda campaigns have blurred the truth about climate change and its causes. This has directly resulted in public confusion and inaction. Unlike smoking, where it was easier to directly link individuals smoking habits to their illnesses, global warming is harder to pin down.

In 1989, as the world's nations began to turn towards working responsibly together to seek to lower carbon output, Exxon Mobile led the creation of the infamous "Global Climate Coalition". Nothing more than a trojan horse, the "Coalition," a disguised industry-led lobbying group, prevented the US from signing the Kyoto Protocol. This tactic was likely responsible for stopping other countries such as China and India, from signing the treaty for fears of being uncompetitive. [6]

After an eight-month-long, in-depth investigation of former Exxon employees,

[5] Neela Banerjee, Lisa Song, and David Hasemyer, "Exxon's Own Research Confirmed Fossil Fuels' Role in Global Warming Decades Ago," Inside Climate News, September 16, 2015. Geoffrey Supran and Naomi Oreskes, "Assessing ExxonMobil's climate change communications (1977-2014)," Environmental Research Letters 12, no. 8 (August 2017).

[6] Shannon Hall, "Exxon Knew about Climate Change almost 40 years ago," Scientific American, October 26, 2015.

to Exxon's management committee: *"In the first place, there is general scientific agreement that the most likely manner in which mankind is influencing the global climate is through carbon dioxide release from the burning of fossil fuels."* [7] He warned them that doubling CO2 gasses in the atmosphere would increase average global temperatures by two or three degrees. This, of course, has already happened.

Herein lies the major cause of global warming. Harmful industries can profit financially versus adopting cleaner, less polluting technologies. This is not a population problem but a systemic economic problem of Western industrial societies.

More recently, a new twist has been added to obfuscate reality, with global and corporate leaders asserting that global warming is directly related to human population. Now that the impacts of global warming, including storms, fires, flooding, and extreme heat events, are becoming harder to ignore - the blame is being pushed onto the general populace to draw attention away from the main offenders.

In actuality, it is not the number of people that is the driver of climate change, but primarily two other factors: highly polluting industries like oil and gas that monopolize the way we create energy and block the way forward of other less polluting methods available (and not just solar and wind), and the misuse of land. For example, cutting forests when we need them to store carbon and

Climate Change Facts

Climate change and increasing CO2 levels are human-caused and dangerous. Here are a few scientific aspects that prove these facts. First, there are three distinct types of carbon isotopes: 14C, 13C, and 12C. The isotope associated with carbon from burning fossil fuels has risen dramatically since the 1900s; meanwhile, the naturally derived isotope associated with carbon created by trees has decreased. [8]

Sequences of annual tree rings going back thousands of years indicate that at no time in the last 10,000 years have the naturally occurring carbon isotope ratios in the atmosphere been as low as they are today. [9] Not only are naturally occurring carbon isotopes falling but so is Earth's atmosphere's oxygen level. Oxygen levels are falling 2,000 times faster over the past 150 years than in the last 800,000 years. [10]

Greenhouse gasses absorb energy and will thus allow less infrared radiation to escape into space. This is exactly what satellites are finding. From 1970 to 1996, satellites discovered that less energy is escaping into space and proved via "direct experimental evidence of a significant increase in the Earth's greenhouse effect." Moreover, if forces outside of the planet predominantly caused global warming—for example, a hotter sun, another oil industry-created myth—then the outer layers of Earth's

[7] Banerjee, Song, and Hasemyer, "Exxon's Own Research Confirmed Fossil Fuels' Role in Global Warming Decades Ago."

[8] M. Stuiver, R.L. Burk, P.D. Quay, "13C/12C ratios in tree rings and the transfer of biospheric carbon to the atmosphere," Journal of Geophysical Research: Atmospheres 89 [7] (December 1984): 11731-11748.

[9] Eric Steig, "How do we know that recent CO2 increases are due to human activities?" RealClimate: Climate science from climate scientists, December 22, 2004, http://www.realclimate.org/index.php/archives/2004/12/how-do-we-know-that-recent-cosub2sub-increases-are-due-to-human-activities-updated/.

[10] Charles Choi, Earth's Atmospheric Oxygen Levels Continue Long Slide, Live Science, September 22, 2016, https://www.livescience.com/56219-earth-atmospheric-oxygen-levels-declining.html accessed on February 2020

[11] J.E. Harries et al., "Increases in greenhouse forcing inferred from the outgoing longwave radiation spectra of the Earth in 1970 and 1997," Nature 410, no. 6828 (2001): 355-357.

"Climate models predict that more carbon dioxide should cause warming in the troposphere but cooling in the stratosphere. This is because the increased "blanketing" effect in the troposphere holds in more heat, allowing less to reach the stratosphere. This would contrast with the expected effect if global warming were caused by the sun, causing warming both in the troposphere and stratosphere. Instead, satellites and weather balloons confirm a cooling stratosphere and warming troposphere, consistent with increased carbon dioxide." [12]

Some "climate change deniers" will rely on ice samples taken from the Vostok core at the Earth's polar region to support their argument that the Earth's present warming trend is a naturally occurring cycle and, is thus, ok? They refer to an ice-drilling project between Russia, the United States, and France at the Russian Vostok station in East Antarctica. This yielded the deepest ice core ever recovered, with layers of ice going back 800,000 years. [13]

While the drilled ice samples show that the Earth has gone through cycles of warming and cooling trends, there have not been periods in Earth's history when temperatures were warmer than they are now. Also, the rate of climate change today is far more rapid than the climate shifts that occurred in the past. The Vostok ice cores show us that the rate of change in CO2 over the past million years is tame compared to today's rapid rate of change. Before the Industrial Revolution, CO2 changed to less than 0.15 ppm per year. [14] Today's rate of change is twenty times faster!

Unfortunately, the earth has been here before - and its not pretty. In the end-Triassic extinction 200 million years ago, CO2 doubled from 2,000 to 4,400 ppm, triggered by massive volcanic eruptions. [15] This happened over the relatively short time of 1,000 to 20,000 years and wiped-out 75 percent of all land species and 95 percent of all marine species. If humankind had been around then, we would have become extinct!

If we compare this event to our present global warming, the rate of change that occurred then is just a fraction of the rate of change occurring now. In April 2020, our planet had 419 ppm of CO2 in the atmosphere, which is rising rapidly! (For updates, go to https://climate.nasa. gov/vital-signs/carbon-dioxide/.)

Already we are observing the beginning of end-Triassic conditions. In that period, oceans became acidic soups devoid of oxygen, suffocating almost all marine life. Unfortunately, dead zones are now appearing in many different locations in our oceans.[16] Extinction events are not something that changes back to safe levels quickly. The end-Triassic extinction showed that it could take millions of years for life to recover and

---

[12] Kevin Trenberth, "Global Warming is Happening," National Center for Atmospheric Research, accessed March 25, 2020.

[13] Peter Rejcek, "Going Deep: Drilling project to retrieve longest ice core ever from South Pole," In-Depth Newsletter, National Science Foundation Ice Core Facility, Spring 2015

[14] Shaun A. Marcott et al., "Centennial-scale changes in the global carbon cycle during the last deglaciation," Nature 514, nos. 616-619 (October 2014).

[15] Morgan F. Schaller, James D. Wright, and Dennis V. Kent, "Atmospheric PCO2 Perturbations Associated with the Central Atlantic Magmatic Province," Science 331, no. 6023 (March 2011): 1404-1409.

[16] Denise Breitburg et al., "Declining oxygen in the global ocean and coastal waters," Science 359, no. 6371 (January 2018).

Time to Turn to Newer Innovative Ways to Generate Energy

For those that choose to ignore the realities of global warming, if we focus alone on the antiquity of our energy industries, they lag far behind new, more sustainable, and less expensive technologies. The design for the combustion engine now used in most vehicles to consume oil and gas is well over 100 years old! Meanwhile, other technology sectors have sped way past these dinosaur technologies. The fact that society is stuck in the same old way of powering our world reflects that our political-economic systems support monopolies and existing industries by blocking new technologies.

For example, patents on alternative energy devices abound, but a large percentage are hidden. This results from the Invention Secrecy Act, which allows the United States Patent Office "USPTO" to keep some patents on lockdown. There are now well over 5,000 patents that are considered secret. Some of these are related to new clean energy devices. Even solar energy and photovoltaic generators were initially in 1971 considered for restriction and secrecy. The Army, the Air Force, and NASA all considered "solar photovoltaic generators" as having military applications for space systems.

In addition, many clean energy companies hide their new findings and technology as "trade secrets." Not only does hiding new technology slow innovation, but keeping it hidden and unobtainable in the face of our global crisis is simply madness. Humanity does not deserve to be trapped in centuries-old technology.

Not only do oil and gas industries pollute the atmosphere, but they also pollute the land and water through their pipeline and tanker oil spills and fracking. We have the wherewithal to invent newer and better alternatives to generate energy. It's time to let go of these ancient, inefficient, and harmful technologies and apply new methods that run far more efficiently and safely.

As if historical records were not dire warnings enough about the impact of increased CO2, we also have to add two other very important trends that are affecting Earth today. These trends were not taking place during the period of the Triassic. We have allowed massive deforestation from clear-cutting, forest fires, and soil and water contamination. Over the past 200 years, humanity has wiped out approximately 50 percent of the Earth's forest cover. [18] Thus, not only are we pumping carbon dioxide into the atmosphere at an alarming rate, but we are also wiping out the very species we need to help regulate our climate. The reality is that humanity has never faced this rapid and devasting change under these dire circumstances, nor has the Earth.

[18] Max Roser, "Forests," Our World in Data, Global Change Data Lab, accessed July 17, 2020, https://ourworldindata.org/forests#global-forest-cover-change-over-the-last-centuries.

world leaders set targets to conserve key habitats, stem pollution, and conduct important ecological research. Yet, eight years later, in 2010, the Convention on Biological Diversity published a Global Biodiversity Outlook with a grim update. The convention's report concluded that:

"The loss of biodiversity is an issue of profound concern for its own sake. Biodiversity also underpins the functioning of ecosystems, which provide a wide range of services to human societies. Its continued loss, therefore, has major implications for current and future human well-being."

This report is a wake-up call and a reason to take action. This is not the time to sit back and think that someone else will save the world. Whether this new era ends well or not depends entirely on us. It is simply not possible to run away from climate change by ignoring it. Nor is it possible to "leave the scene." There is only one Earth.

Informing and educating others about the truth that global warming exists as well as sharing personal stories of loss caused by it can help us unite into a shared understanding of what is really happening in our world. We must also take action. Supporting and electing political candidates that platform a green agenda, reign in fossil fuels, and roll out and support alternative energy programs is a requisite for our survival.

CONCLUSION

The global extinction rate is at least tens of hundreds of times higher than usual and still accelerating, threatening to eclipse some of Earth's most significant mass die-offs. One in six U.S. tree species is threatened with extinction. Yet, many forest management agencies and professionals worldwide overlook the importance of trees and forest lands that supply Earth's oxygen, feed its animals, and store more carbon than humanity will emit in 10 years (Kayler et al., 2017).

Although forest lands are facing threats never seen in previous generations, out of date and, in some cases, even harmful forest management practices are being applied. Policy measures and on-site procedures reflect misunderstandings about the importance of our natural world and the catastrophic climate changes we now face.

Increased logging of forest lands is not only a threat to biodiversity and the soil and atmospheric conditions necessary for healthy forests, but it can even cause fires to move more quickly and ferociously. Modern "firenados" are driven by rising global temperatures and are caused primarily by human ignition.

Present policies and funding priorities are misaligned due to reliance on industry lobbying and economics. Policies must focus on stopping fires before they start, protecting our valuable forest lands, improving communication systems, and subsidizing homeowners for fireproofing their buildings. Forest management officials must recognize the importance of forests and their unique functions and ecological roles. A healthy forest supports biodiversity, slows wildfires, prevents flooding, and provides a healing and inspiring place for young and old.

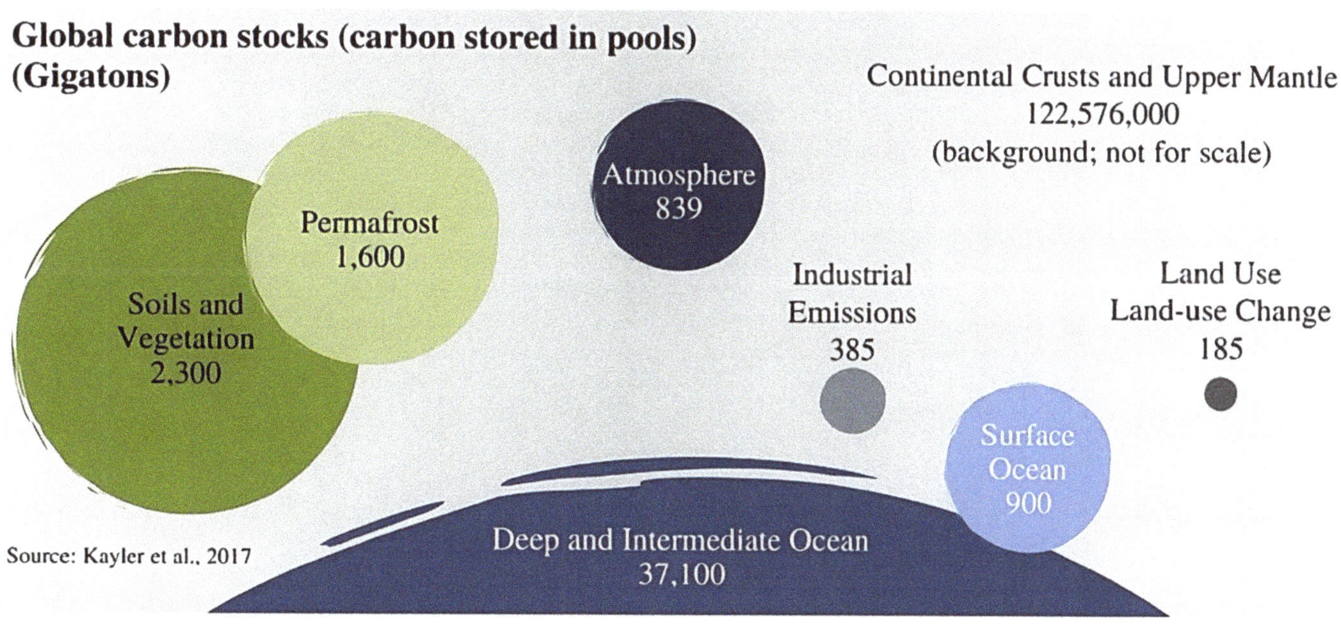

APPENDIX A: Letter from Scientists to President Biden

Open Letter to President Biden and Members of Congress from Scientists: It is essential to Remove Climate-Harming Logging and Fossil Fuel Provisions from Reconciliation and Infrastructure Bills

November 4, 2021

Dear President Biden and Members of Congress,

As scientists with expertise in ecology, forest management, biodiversity, and climate change, we are writing to urge you to remove from the Budget Reconciliation and Infrastructure provisions that promote logging and fossil fuels because such measures will only make worse the global climate and biodiversity crises. As an initial matter, we note that, even under optimistic expert estimates, the clean energy provisions in these bills are insufficiently bold and would, by themselves, only achieve a fraction of what we would need to reach the Administration's minimum climate crisis mitigation target of a 50% reduction in annual U.S. greenhouse gas emissions from 2005 levels by 2030.[1] Making matters worse, the bills contain numerous logging provisions that would dramatically increase annual carbon emissions from logging for lumber, forest biomass energy, and wood pellets on public and private forestlands nationwide, which would undermine natural climate solutions and our forests' carbon storage and sink capacities. The Reconciliation Bill is in jeopardy unless the cost can be reduced. Removing these compromising logging provisions and the subsidies for logging, bioenergy and fossil fuels would help accomplish that goal.

As hundreds of climate and forest scientists warned Congress last year, logging in U.S. forests emits 723 million tons of uncounted CO_2 into our atmosphere each year—more than 10 times the amount emitted by wildfires and tree mortality from insects combined.[2] Greenhouse gas emissions from logging in U.S. forests are now comparable to the annual CO_2 emissions from U.S. coal burning, and annual emissions from the building sector.[3] Most of the carbon in trees removed from forests through logging is emitted almost immediately, as branches and tree tops are burned at biomass energy facilities, and mill residues are burned at the sawmills, typically for energy production[4]—emitting more CO_2 than burning coal, for equal energy produced.[5] Logging conducted as commercial "thinning," under the rubric of fire management, emits about three times more CO_2 than wildfire alone.[6]

The Reconciliation Bill currently contains $14 billion in new subsidies for logging on federal public lands—more than double existing levels—as well as billions in new logging subsidies on private forestlands. The Reconciliation Bill further proposes nearly $1 billion in new subsidies for forest biomass energy, wood pellet facilities, and mass timber (cross-laminated timber) under the heading of "wood innovation." This ignores the advice of hundreds of climate and forest scientists who have previously informed Congress that these industries substantially increase emissions and worsen the climate crisis.[7]

The Infrastructure Bill includes a legislative mandate for 30 million acres of additional logging on federal public lands over the next 15 years, in addition to misdirecting billions of dollars in new subsidies for the fossil fuel industry and an exemption from environmental analysis for new oil and gas pipelines across federal lands. It also includes provisions that would roll back the National Environmental Policy Act by creating new "categorical exclusion" exemptions from environmental analysis and disclosure of adverse impacts of this logging on our climate and forest biodiversity, while eliminating the public's right to file administrative objections on logging proposals. Further, the Infrastructure bill includes $400 million for destructive post-fire clearcutting on public lands, and $400 million in new subsidies for forest biomass and wood pellet facilities, which not only harm our climate and forest ecosystems but also disproportionately adversely affect communities of color with increased particulate and toxic pollution.[8] In addition, there are $18 billion in new subsidies in the bill for the forest biomass/pellet and fossil fuel industries to promote carbon capture and storage (CCS) and biomass energy with carbon capture and storage (BECCS), and construction of a massive network of CO_2 pipelines. Hundreds of climate scientists, and conservation and environmental justice organizations, have decried this as a false climate solution that can actually increase net carbon emissions and energy consumption while increasing pollution in communities of color.[9]

In both bills, logging provisions are promoted as wildfire management and climate solutions measures, but commercial logging conducted under the guise of "thinning" and "fuel reduction" typically removes mature, fire-resistant trees that are needed for forest resilience. We have watched as one large wildfire after another has swept through tens of thousands of acres where commercial thinning had previously occurred due to extreme fire weather driven by climate change. Removing trees can alter a forest's microclimate, and can often increase fire intensity.[10] In contrast, forests protected from logging, and those with high carbon biomass and carbon storage, more often burn at equal or lower intensities when fires do occur.[11]

We urge Congress to move in the opposite direction by shifting from more logging toward natural climate solutions that store carbon in mature and older forests and allow naturally regenerating forests to continue growing for greater carbon accumulation. For example, protecting U.S. federal public forestlands from logging would not only reduce direct carbon emissions but would also increase annual drawdown of atmospheric CO_2 by 84 million tons per year.[12] We do not wish to follow our Canadian neighbors where some of their managed forests have become a source of emissions because they followed many of the proposed policies in these Bills. There is a path toward meeting the vital 2030 climate crisis mitigation goals, but not with the Reconciliation and Infrastructure Bills as currently written.

We need the Administration and Congress to enact policies that will substantially *reduce* annual greenhouse gas emissions from logging, and from fossil fuels, and increase accumulation of carbon in our forests. The recent IPCC AR6 report released in August makes clear the urgent need to reduce emissions by at least half by 2030 to avoid large increases of devastating heat domes, prolonged droughts, wildfires that can impact communities, intense precipitation events, and catastrophic storms. The logging and fossil fuel subsidies and policies in the Reconciliation and Infrastructure Bills will only intensify the rate and intensity of our changing climate.

Lead Signatories

** Affiliations listed for identification purposes only*

William R. Moomaw, Ph.D.
Emeritus Professor

2

The Fletcher School Co-director Global Development and Environment Institute Tufts University
Medford, MA, USA

Chad T. Hanson, Ph.D., Forest Ecologist
Earth Island Institute
Berkeley, CA, USA

Dominick A. DellaSala, Ph.D., Chief Scientist
Wild Heritage, a project of the Earth Island Institute
Talent, OR, USA

James E. Hansen, Ph.D.
Director, Program in Climate Science, Awareness and Solutions
Earth Institute, Columbia University
New York, NY

Pushker A. Kharecha, Ph.D.
Climate Scientist and Deputy Director
Climate Science, Awareness, and Solutions Program
Columbia University Earth Institute, New York, NY

Beverly Law, Ph.D., Professor Emeritus, Global Change Bio. and Terrestrial Systems Science
Department of Forest Ecosystems & Society Oregon State University
Corvallis, OR

William Ripple, Ph.D.
Distinguished Professor of Ecology
Oregon State University, Corvallis, OR

Peter H. Raven, Ph.D.
President Emeritus, Missouri Botanical Garden George Engelmann Professor of Botany
Emeritus, Washington University in St. Louis
St. Louis, MO

Thomas Lovejoy, Ph.D.
Professor, Environmental Science and Policy George Mason University
Fairfax City, VA
Senior Fellow, United Nations Foundation

William H. Schlesinger, Ph.D.
James B. Duke Professor of Biogeochemistry Dean (Em.) the School of the Env.,
Duke Univ. President (Em.), the Cary Inst. of Eco. Studies
Millbrook, NY

William L. Baker, Ph.D.

3

Emeritus Professor
Program in Ecology
University of Wyoming
Laramie, WY 82071

John Talberth, Ph.D.
Center for Sustainable Economy
Portland, OR

Michael Dorsey, Ph.D., M.F.S., M.A.
M.F.S., Yale University, School of Forestry
M.A., The Johns Hopkins Univ., Anthropology
Ph.D., University of Michigan, School for Environment and Sustainability

Mary S. Booth, Ph.D., Director
Partnership for Policy Integrity
Pelham, MA

Christopher Neil, Ph.D., Senior Scientist
Woodwell Climate Research Center
Falmouth, MA

Wayne S. Walker, Ph.D., Carbon Program Director
Woodwell Climate Research Center
Falmouth, MA

Jennifer Francis, Ph.D., Acting Deputy Director, Senior Scientist
Woodwell Climate Research Center
Falmouth, MA

Susan M. Natali, Ph.D., Arctic Program Director, Senior Scientist
Woodwell Climate Research Center
Falmouth, MA

Marcia N. Macedo, Ph.D., Water Program Director, Associate Scientist
Woodwell Climate Research Center
Falmouth, MA

Derek Lee, Ph.D.
Associate Professor
Penn State University, PA

Monica Bond, Ph.D.
Wild Nature Institute
Concord, NH

4

Robert L. Beschta, Ph.D.
Professor Emeritus
Forest Ecosystems and Society, Oregon State University
Corvallis, OR 97333

Thomas T. Veblen, Ph.D.
Distinguished Professor, Emeritus
University of Colorado Boulder, CO

Stuart Pimm, Ph.D.
Doris Duke Chair of Conservation Duke University
Durham, NC

Mark E. Harmon, Ph.D., Professor Emeritus
Department of Forest Ecosystems & Society
Oregon State University
Corvallis, OR

Anne H. Ehrlich, Ph.D.
Center for Conservation Biology Stanford University
Palo Alto, CA

Paul R. Ehrlich, Ph.D., Professor Emeritus, Biology Stanford University
President, Center for Conservation Biology
Palo Alto, CA

Steven Green, Ph.D.
Senior Professor Emeritus
University of Miami, Coral Gables, FL

Tonja Chi, M.S., Wildlife Ecologist
Campbell, California

Maya Khosla, M.S.
Wildlife Biologist and Toxicologist
Rohnert Park, CA

Richard W. Halsey, M.A.
California Chaparral Institute

Bryant Baker, M.S., Conservation Director
Los Padres ForestWatch
Santa Barbara, CA

Shaye Wolf, Ph.D.
Climate Science Director

5

Center for Biological Diversity

Eric Chivian, M.D.
Founder and Former Director, Center for Health and the Global Environment
Harvard Medical School
Boston, Massachusetts

Gregory F. Grether, Ph.D.
Professor of Ecology and Evolutionary Biology
University of California, Los Angeles

Bruce G. Baldwin, Ph.D.
W. L. Jepson Professor & Curator
Department of Integrative Biology and Jepson Herbarium
University of California, Berkeley

John P. O'Brien, Ph.D., Climate Scientist
National Center for Atmospheric Research
Boulder, CO

A. Scott Denning, Ph.D.
Monfort Professor of Atmospheric Science
Colorado State University and
Coleman P. Burke Distinguished Visiting Professor
Yale School of the Environment

Scott Goetz, Ph.D.
Regents Professor of Earth Observation & Ecological Informatics
School of Informatics, Computing and Cyber Systems
Northern Arizona University, Flagstaff AZ
Science Lead, NASA Arctic Boreal Vulnerability Experiment
Deputy PI for Science, NASA Global Ecosystem Dynamics Investigation

John Sterman, Ph.D.
Professor and Director
MIT Systems Dynamics Group
Sloan School of Management
Massachusetts Institute of Technology
Cambridge, MA

Juliette N. Rooney-Varga, Ph.D.
Director, Climate Change Initiative
Professor, Environmental Science
Co-Director, Rist Institute for Sustainability and Energy
Lowell, MA

6

(Signatures continue for 18 more pages in the original letter.)

REFERENCES

Abatzoglou, J. T., & Williams, A. P. (2016). Impact of anthropogenic climate change on wildfire across western US forests. Proceedings of the National Academy of Sciences, 113(42), 11770–11775. https://doi.org/10.1073/pnas.1607171113

Aldous, P. (2018). Why California Can't Chainsaw Its Way Out of a Raging Inferno. Buzzfeed News. https://www.buzzfeednews.com/article/peteraldhous/logging-forest-california-wildfires

Alley, R.B., Berntsen, T., Bindoff, N.L.,...& Zwiers, F. (2018). A report of Working Group I of the Intergovernmental Panel on Climate Change: Summary for Policymakers. Intergovernmental Panel on Climate Change. https://www.ipcc.ch/site/assets/uploads/2018/02/ar4-wg1-spm-1.pdf

Ansley, J.S., & Battles, J.J. (1998). Forest composition, structure, and change in an old-growth mixed conifer forest in the northern Sierra Nevada. Journal of the Torrey Botanical Society, 125(4), 297-308. https://www.sierraforestlegacy.org/Resources/Conservation/FireForestEcology/ThreatenedHabitats/OldGrowthForests/OGF-Ansley98.pdf

Arthur, D. (2020). 'Pretty insane': Creek Fire fueled by extreme behavior, including two 'firenadoes.' Visalia Times-Delta. https://www.visaliatimesdelta.com/story/news/2020/09/06/creek-fire-update-ca-firenadoes-fueled-extreme-behavior-weather/5736222002/

Asner, G.P., Brodrick, P.G., Anderson, C.B.,...& Martin, R.E. (2015). Progressive forest canopy water loss during the 2012-2015 California drought. Proceedings of the National Academy of Sciences, 113(2), E249-E255. https://doi.org/10.1073/pnas.1523397113

Balch, J.K., Bradley, B.A., Abatzoglou, J.T.,...& Mahood, A.L. (2017). Human-started wildfires expand the fire niche across the United States. Proceedings of the National Academy of Sciences, 114(11), 2946-2951. https://doi.org/10.1073/pnas.1617394114

Ballaré, C. L., Rousseau, M. C., Searles, P. S., Zaller, J. G., Giordano, C. V., Robson, T. M., Caldwell, M. M., Sala, O. E., & Scopel, A. L. (2001). Impacts of solar ultraviolet-B radiation on Tierra del Fuego (southern Argentina) terrestrial ecosystems: An overview of recent progress. Journal of Photochemistry and Photobiology B: Biology, 62(1-2), 67–77. https://doi.org/10.1016/s1011-1344(01)00152-x

Barrett, S. W., T. W. Swetnam, and W. L. Baker. (2005). Indian fire use: deflating the legend. Fire Management Today, 65(3), 31-34. https://www.researchgate.net/publication/228116861_Indian_fire_use_deflating_the_legend Bartholomew, A. (2003). Hidden Nature: The Startling Insights of Viktor Schauberger. Floris Books.

Bedsworth, L., Cayan, D., Franco, G., Fisher, L., & Ziaja, S. (2018). Statewide Summary Report. California's Fourth Climate Change Assessment. https://www.energy.ca.gov/sites/default/files/2019-11/Statewide_Reports-SUM-CCCA4-2018-013_Statewide_Summary_Report_ADA.pdf

Benca, Jeffrey P., Duijnstee, Ivo A., & Looy, Cindy V. (2018). UV-B–induced forest sterility: Implications of ozone shield failure in Earth's largest extinction. Science Advances, 4(2).https://www.science.org/doi/10.1126/sciadv.1700618

Bello, C., Galetti, M., Pizo, M.A.,...& Jordano, P. (2015). Defaunation affects carbon storage in tropical forests. Science Advances, 1(11). https://www.science.org/doi/10.1126/sciadv.1501105

Bernes, C., Jonsson, B. G., Junninen, K., & Lõhmus, A. (2015). What is the impact of active management on biodiversity in boreal and temperate forests set aside for conservation or restoration? A systematic map. Environmental Evidence, 4(25). https://doi.org/10.1186/s13750-015-0050-7

Biello, D. (2008). One Quarter of World's Mammals Face Extinction. Scientific American. https://www.scientificamerican.com/article/one-quarter-of-worlds-mammals-face-extinction/#:~:text=The%20resu lts%2C%20published%20in%20Science,all%20mammal%20species%20are%20declining

Borunda, A. (2020). The science connecting wildfires to climate change. National Geographic. https://www.nationalgeographic.com/science/article/climate-change-increases-risk-fires-western-us

Bradley, C. M., Hanson, C. T., & DellaSala, D. A. (2016). Does increased forest protection correspond to higher fire severity in frequent Western United States fire forests? Ecosphere, 7(10): e01492. https://doi.org/10.1002/ecs2.1492

Bradshaw, S.D., Dixon, K. W., Lambers, H., & Cross, A. T. (2018). Understanding the long-term impact of prescribed burning in Mediterranean-climate biodiversity hotspots, focusing on south-western Australia. International Journal of Wildland Fire, 27(10), 643-657. https://www.publish.csiro.au/wf/WF18067

Briggs, Helen. (2020). Wildlife in 'catastrophic decline' due to human destruction, scientists warn. BBC News. https://www.bbc.com/news/science-environment-54091048

Brown, M. J., Parker, G. G., & Posner, N. E. (1994). A Survey of Ultraviolet-B Radiation in Forests. Journal of Ecology, 82(4), 843–854. https://doi.org/10.2307/2261448

Cabrol, N.A., Feister, U., Häder, D.,...& Klein, A. (2014). Record solar UV irradiance in the tropical Andes. Frontiers in Environmental Science, 2, 19. https://www.frontiersin.org/articles/10.3389/fenvs.2014.00019/full

California Department of Fish and Wildlife. (2019). Biodiversity - The Variety of Life on Earth. California Department of Fish and Wildlife. https://wildlife.ca.gov/Biodiversity

California Native Grassland Association. (2021). Grasslands Conservation. California Native Grassland Association. https://www.cnga.org/Conservation

Calkin, D. E., Cohen, J. D., Finney, M. A., & Thompson, M. P. (2013). How risk management can prevent future wildfire disasters in the wildland-urban interface. Proceedings of the National Academy of Sciences, 111(2), 746–751. https://doi.org/10.1073/pnas.1315088111

Campbell, J.L., Donato, D., Azuma, D., & Law, B. (2007). Pyrogenic carbon emission from a large wildfire in Oregon, United States. Journal of Geophysical Research, 112, GO4014. https://doi.org/10.1029/2007JG000451

Campbell, J.L., Harmon, M.E., & Mitchell, S.R. (2011). Can fuel-reduction treatments increase forest carbon storage in the western US by reducing future fire emissions? Frontiers in Ecology and the Environment, 10(2), 83-90. https://doi.org/10.1890/110057

Cannon, C.H., Piovesan, G. & Munné-Bosch, S. (2022). Old trees are life history lottery winners and vital evolutionary resources for long-term adaptive capacity. Nature Plants 8, 136–145. https://doi.org/10.1038/s41477-021-01088-5

Center for Biological Diversity. (2020). Built to Burn: California's Wildlands Developments Are Playing With Fire Bold Land-use Reforms Needed Now to Ensure Safer, Sustainable Future [report]. Center for Biological Diversity. https://www.biologicaldiversity.org/programs/urban/pdfs/Built-to-Burn-California-Wildfire-Report-Center-Biologic al-Diversity.pdf

Centers for Disease Control and Prevention. (2015, June 2). Rates of new melanomas – deadly skin cancers – have doubled over the last three decades [press release]. Centers for Disease Control and Prevention. https://www.cdc.gov/media/releases/2015/p0602-melanoma-cancer.html

Choi, C. (2016, September 22). Earth's Atmospheric Oxygen Levels Continue Long Slide. Live Science. https://www.livescience.com/56219-earth-atmospheric-oxygen-levels-declining.html

Choi, C.Q. (2009). The Lost Forests of America. Live Science. ttps://www.livescience.com/7725-lost-forests-america.html

Christensen, G.A., Campbell, S.J., & Fried, J.S. (2008). California's forest resources, 2001-2005: five-year Forest Inventory and Analysis Report. Pacific Northwest Research Station, 183 p. https://doi.org/10.2737/PNW-GTR-763

Chung, E. (2017). Some forests need to grow back after wildfires, research finds. CBC News. https://www.cbc.ca/news/science/forests-wildfires-1.4444998

Clugston, Gina. (2015, October 21). Residents Can Face Fines For Illegal Burns. Sierra News Online. https://sierranewsonline.com/residents-can-face-fines-for-illegal-burns/

Columbia Climate School. (2016, October 10). Climate Change Has Doubled Western U.S. Forest Fires, Says Study. Columbia Climate School. Columbia University. https://www.earth.columbia.edu/articles/view/3343

Columbia Climate School. (2010, September 7). Irrigation's Cooling Effects May Mask Warming--For Now Columbia Climate School: The Earth Institute. Columbia University. https://www.earth.columbia.edu/articles/view/2726

Cornwall, W. (2015). California's Forests: Where Have All the Big Trees Gone? National Geographic.https://www.nationalgeographic.com/science/article/150119-california-forests-shrinking-climate-droug ht-science

Costa, H., et al. (2022). Dead zone. National Geographic. https://education.nationalgeographic.org/resource/dead-zone

Cotton, S. (2015). Isoprene. Education in Chemistry. Royal Society of Chemistry. https://edu.rsc.org/magnificent-molecules/isoprene/2000024.article

Crimes and Punishments, Cal. Penal Code § 452 (1872). California Legislative Information. https://leginfo.legislature.ca.gov/faces/codes_displaySection.xhtml?sectionNum=452.&lawCode=PEN

Davis, M., Faurby, S., & Svenning, J.C. (2018). Mammal diversity will take millions of years to recover from the current biodiversity crisis—the National Academy of Sciences proceedings.https://doi.org/10.1073/pnas.1804906115

Dean, J.C., Kusaka, R., Walsh, P.S., Allais, F., & Zwier, T.S. (2014). Plant Sunscreens in the UV-B: Ultraviolet Spectroscopy of Jet-Cooled Sinapoyl Malate, Sinapic Acid, and Sinapate Ester Derivatives. American Chemical Society, 136(42), 14780-14795. https://doi.org/10.1021/ja5059026

Depro, B.M., Murray, B.C., Alig, R.L., & Shanks, A. (2008). Public land, timber harvests, and climate mitigation: quantifying carbon sequestration potential on U.S. public timberlands. Forest Ecology and Management, 255, 1122-1134. https://www.fs.usda.gov/treesearch/pubs/33137

Ferguson, S. C., Dahale, A., Shotorban, B., & Mahalingam, S. (2013). The role of moisture on combustion of pyrolysis gases in wildland fires. Combust. Sci. Technol, 185(3), 435–453. https://www.fs.usda.gov/treesearch/pubs/43414

Fitzsimons, T., & Helsel, P. (2020). A woman who died in California fires was ready to flee but stayed because of 'erroneous information.' NBC News. https://www.nbcnews.com/news/us-news/man-woman-who-died-california-fires-were-ready-flee-stayed-n1240200

Forzieri, G., Dakos, V., McDowell, N.G., Ramdane, A., & Cescatti, A. (2022). Emerging signals of declining forest resilience under climate change. Nature, 608, 534-539. https://www.nature.com/articles/s41586-022-04959-9

Fraser, W., Watson, J., Sephton, M.A., & Self, S. (2011). UV-B absorbing pigments in spores: Biochemical responses to shade in a high-latitude birch forest and implications for sporopollenin-based proxies of past environmental change. Polar Research, 30, 8312. https://doi.org/10.3402/polar.v30i0.8312

Gee, A. (2021, March 10). Is this the end of forests as we know them? The Guardian. https://www.theguardian.com/environment/2021/mar/10/is-this-the-end-of-forests-as-weve-known-them?fbclid=I wAR3Pp6qykyy-3XYVWrvTR5eU1v8qwrlVoQCvfJG32Krv5CcQ-rWvHkbcZPE

Gonsalves, L., Law, B., & Blakey, R. (2018). Experimental evaluation of the initial effects of large-scale thinning on the structure and biodiversity of river red gum (Eucalyptus camaldulensis) forests. Wildlife Research, 45(5), 397-410. https://www.publish.csiro.au/wr/wr17168

Grant, R.H., Heisler, G.M., Gao, W. (2002). Estimation of Pedestrian Level UV Exposure Under Trees.Photochemistry and Photobiology, 75(4), 369-376. https://onlinelibrary.wiley.com/doi/abs/10.1562/0031-8655(2002)0750369EOPLUE2.0.CO2

Green, E., McRae, L., Harfoot, M., Hill, S., Simonson, W., & Baldwin-Cantello, W. (2019). Below the Canopy. World Wide Fund for Nature.https://c402277.ssl.cf1.rackcdn.com/publications/1250/files/original/BelowTheCanopy_Full_Report.pdf?15657062 51

Griffin, D., & Anchukaitis, K. J. (2014). How unusual is the 2012–2014 California drought? Geophysical Research Letters, 41(24), 9017-9023. https://agupubs.onlinelibrary.wiley.com/doi/abs/10.1002/2014GL062433

Gutierrez, I. (2020). California's Role Fighting the Global Biodiversity Crisis. NRDC. https://www.nrdc.org/experts/irene-gutierrez/californias-role-fighting-global-biodiversity-crisis

Häder, D-P., Helbling, E.W., Williamson, C.E., & Worrest, R.C. (2011). Effects of UV radiation on aquatic ecosystems and interactions with climate change. Photochem Photobiol Sci., 10(2), 242-60. https://pubmed.ncbi.nlm.nih.gov/21253662/

Hanson, C. T., & DellaSala D. A. (2022). Logging makes forests and homes more vulnerable to wildfires. The Hill. https://thehill.com/blogs/congress-blog/energy-environment/590415-logging-makes-forests-and-homes-more-vuln arable

Hanson, C.T. (2021) Is "Fuel Reduction" Justified as Fire Management in Spotted Owl Habitat? Birds, 2(4), 395–403. https://doi.org/10.3390/birds2040029

Hantson, S., Andela, N., Goulden, M.L., & Randerson, J.T. (2022). Human-ignited fires result in more extreme fire behavior and ecosystem impacts. Nature Communications, 13, 2717. https://doi.org/10.1038/s41467-022-30030-2

Harmon, M.E., Harmon, J.M., & Ferrell, W.K. (1996). Modeling carbon stores in Oregon and Washington forest products: 1900-1992. Climatic Change, 33, 521-550. https://doi.org/10.1007/BF00141703

Harries, J. E., Brindley, H. E., Sagoo, P. J., & Bantges, R. J. (2001). Increases in greenhouse forcing were inferred from the outgoing longwave radiation spectra of the Earth in 1970 and 1997. Nature, 410(6826), 355–357. https://doi.org/10.1038/35066553

Harris, N.L., Hagen, S.C., Saatchi, S.S.,...& Yu, Y. (2016). Attribution of net carbon change by disturbance type across the conterminous United States forest lands. Carbon Balance and Management, 11, 24. https://doi.org/10.1186/s13021-016-0066-5

Hartmann, H., Bastos, A., Das, A. J., Esquivel-Muelbert, A., Hammond, W. M., Martínez-Vilalta, J., McDowell, N. G., Powers, J. S., Pugh, T. A.M., Ruthrof, K. X., & Allen, C. D. (2022). Climate Change Risks to Global Forest Health: Emergence of Unexpected Events of Elevated Tree Mortality Worldwide. Annual Review of Plant Biology, 73(1), 673-702. https://www.annualreviews.org/doi/abs/10.1146/annurev-arplant-102820-012804

Heisler, G.M., & Grant, R.H. (2000). Ultraviolet radiation in urban ecosystems with consideration of effects on human health. Urban Ecosystems, 4, 193-229. https://link.springer.com/article/10.1023/A:1012210710900

Hoover, K., & Hanson, L. A. (2022, August 1). Wildfire Statistics. Congressional Research Service. https://sgp.fas.org/crs/misc/IF10244.pdf

Huang, X., Hall, A. D., & Berg, N. (2018). Anthropogenic Warming Impacts on Today's Sierra Nevada Snowpack and Flood Risk. Geophysical Research Letters, 45(12), 6215-6222. https://doi.org/10.1029/2018GL077432

Insurance Information Institute. (2021). Facts + statistics: Wildfires. Insurance Information Institute.https://www.iii.org/fact-statistic/facts-statistics-wildfires

Insurance Information Institute. (2021). Insurance Fact Book 2021. Insurance Information Institute. https://www.iii.org/sites/default/files/docs/pdf/insurance_factbook_2021.pdf

IPCC, 2019: Summary for Policymakers. In: Climate Change and Land: an IPCC Special Report on Climate Change, desertification, Land Degradation, sustainable land management, Food Security, and greenhouse gas fluxes in Terrestrial Ecosystems [P.R. Shukla, J. Skea, E. Calvo Buendia, V. Masson-Delmotte, H.- O. Pörtner, D.C. Roberts, P. Zhai, R. Slade, S. Connors, R. van Diemen, M. Ferrat, E. Haughey, S. Luz, S. Neogi, M. Pathak, J. Petzold, J. Portugal Pereira, P. Vyas, E. Huntley, K. Kissick, M. Belkacemi, J. Malley, (eds.)]. https://www.ipcc.ch/srccl/chapter/summary-for-policymakers/

Jakobs, J. (2020). California Forests 80%-600% Denser Than 150 Years Ago, UC Researcher Says Biomass Is One of the Answers. GVWire. https://gvwire.com/2020/09/15/california-forests-80-600-denser-than-150-years-ago-uc-researcher-says-biomass-i s-one-of-the-answers/

Jędrczak, A., Królik, D., Sędecka, Z., Myszograj, S., Suchowska-Kisielewicz, M., & Bojarski, J. (2014). Testing of Co-Fermentation of Poultry Manure and Corn Silage. Civil and Environmental Engineering Reports, 13(2), 31-47. https://doi.org/10.2478/ceer-2014-0013

Johnson, H., McGhee, E., & Mejia, M.C. (2022). California's Population. Public Policy Institute of California.https://www.ppic.org/publication/californias-population/#:~:text=With%20over%2039%20million%20people,45% 20million%20people%20by%202050.

Joosse, T. (2020). Human-sparked wildfires are more destructive than those caused by nature. Science. https://www.science.org/content/article/human-sparked-wildfires-are-more-destructive-those-caused-nature

Kamrul, H., Abul, A. K., Yeamin, H., & Tareq, A. (2021). Wildfire in Australia during 2019-2020, Its Impact on Health, Biodiversity and Environment with Some Proposals for Risk Management: A Review. Journal of Environmental Protection, 12(6). https://www.scirp.org/journal/paperinformation.aspx?paperid=110099

Kaplan, S. (2022, July 15). Scientists rush to save 1000-year-old trees on the brink of death. The New York Times. https://www.washingtonpost.com/climate-environment/2022/07/14/these-trees-have-survived-1000-years-can-the y-survive-climate-change/

Kataria, S., Jajoo, A., & Guruprasad, K. N. (2014). Impact of increasing ultraviolet-B (UV-B) radiation on photosynthetic processes. Journal of photochemistry and photobiology. B, Biology, 137, 55–66. https://doi.org/10.1016/j.jphotobiol.2014.02.004

Kayler, Z.; Janowiak, M.; Swanston, C. (2017). Global Carbon. U.S. Department of Agriculture, Forest Service,Climate Change Resource Center. https://www.fs.usda.gov/ccrc/topics/global-carbon

Klein, K. (2017, December 12). Didn't Check Before You Burned? You Could End Up In This Class. KVPR News. https://www.kvpr.org/health/2017-12-12/didnt-check-before-you-burned-you-could-end-up-in-this-class

Kujawski, R. (2011). Long-term Drought Effects on Trees and Shrubs. UMass Extension Landscape, Nursery, and Urban Forestry Program. https://ag.umass.edu/landscape/fact-sheets/long-term-drought-effects-on-trees-shrubs

Lagergren, F., Lankreijer, H., Kučera, J., & Cienciala, E. (2008). Thinning effects on pine-spruce forest transpiration in central Sweden. Forest Ecology and Management, 255(7), 2312-2323. https://doi.org/10.1016/j.foreco.2007.12.047.

Langham, G., Schuetz, J., Soykan, C.,...Distler, T. (2014). Audubon's Birds and Climate Change Report: A Primer for Practitioners. National Audubon Society. http://climate.audubon.org/sites/default/files/Audubon-Birds-Climate-Report-v1.2.pdf

Larvae, K., Moody, T., Axelson, J., Fettig, C., & Cafferata, P. (2019). Synthesis of Research into the Long-Term Outlook for Sierra Nevada Forests Following the Current Bark Beetle Epidemic. USDA Forest Service. https://www.fs.usda.gov/treesearch/pubs/58894

Lees, A. (2022). Global bird populations steadily decline. Cornell Chronicle. https://news.cornell.edu/stories/2022/05/global-bird-populations-steadily-decline

Library of Congress. (2002). California as I Saw It: First-Person Narratives of California's Early Years, 1849 to 1900. https://www.loc.gov/collections/california-first-person-narratives/articles-and-essays/early-california-history/firstpeoples-of-california/

Lindsey, R. (2020). How do we know the build-up of carbon dioxide in the atmosphere is caused by humans? NOAA Climate. https://www.climate.gov/news-features/climate-qa/how-do-we-know-build-carbon-dioxide-atmosphere-caused-humans

Lindsey, R., & Dahlman, L. (2022). Climate Change: Global Temperature. NOAA Climate. https://www.climate.gov/news-features/understanding-climate/climate-change-global-temperature#:~:text=June% 2028%2C%202022-,Highlights,based%20on%20NOAA's%20temperature%20data.

Lott, T. (2020, May 11). Insects Feed Baby Birds. Clemson Cooperative Extension Home and Garden Information Center. Clemson University,https://hgic.clemson.edu/insects-feed-baby-birds/#:~:text=You%20may%20be%20surprised%20to,but%20caterpill ars%20are%20particularly%20important.

Luo, J., Liu, Y., Yang, S.,...& Han, K. (2017). Ultrafast Barrierless Photoisomerization and Strong Ultraviolet Absorption of Photoproducts in Plant Sunscreens. The Journal of Physical Chemistry Letters, 8(5), 1025-1030. https://pubs.acs.org/doi/abs/10.1021/acs.jpclett.7b00083

Lutz, J. A., Furniss, T. J., Johnson, D. J., Davies, S. J., Allen, D., Alonso, A., et al. (2018). Global importance of large-diameter trees. Glob. Ecol. Biogeogr. 27(7), 849–864. https://onlinelibrary.wiley.com/doi/abs/10.1111/geb.12747

Ma, S., Concilio, A., Oakley, B., North, M., & Chen, J. (2010). Spatial variability in microclimate in a mixed-conifer forest before and after thinning and burning treatments. Forest Ecology and Management, 259(5), 904-915. https://www.sciencedirect.com/science/article/abs/pii/S0378112709008615

MacCleery, D.W. (2011). American Forests: A History of Resiliency and Recovery. Forest History Society.https://foresthistory.org/wp-content/uploads/2016/12/American_Forests.pdf

Mader, S. (2007, August 23). CLIMATE PROJECT: Carbon Sequestration and Storage by California Forests and Forest Products. Technical Memorandum. http://featherriver.org/_db/files/194_Carbon-Sequestion-and-Storage-by-CA-Forests-and-Forest-Products.pdf

Marcott, S.A., Bauska, T.K., Buizert, C.,...& Brook, E.J. (2014). Centennial-scale changes in the global carbon cycle during the last deglaciation. Nature, 514, 616-619. https://doi.org/10.1038/nature13799

McCann, H., & Van Butsic. (2021, July 12). How Wood Products Could Lower the Cost of Forest Management. Public Policy Institute of California. https://www.ppic.org/blog/how-wood-products-could-lower-the-cost-of-forest-management/

Molnar, C., & Gair, J. (2015). Concepts of Biology - 1st Canadian Edition. BCcampus. https://opentextbc.ca/biology/chapter/22-4-nitrogenous-wastes/

Moomaw, W.R., Masino, S.A., & Faison, E.K. (2019). Intact Forests in the United States: Proforestation Mitigates Climate Change and Serves the Greatest Good. Frontiers in Forests and Global Change. https://www.frontiersin.org/articles/10.3389/ffgc.2019.00027/full

Mustoe, S. (2021, February 1). The massive impact of animals on forest nutrients. Wildlife in the Balance.https://simonmustoe.blog/the-massive-impact-of-animals-on-forest-nutrients/

National Parks Service. (2022). Indigenous Fire Practices Shape our Land. https://www.nps.gov/subjects/fire/indigenous-fire-practices-shape-our-land.htm#:~:text=Native%20 Americans%2C%20Alaska%20Natives%2C%20and,the%20risk%20of%20catastrophic%20wildfires.

National Parks Service. (2021, March 3). Sequoia and Kings Canyon National Parks Hosted 1.2 Million Visitors in 2020 35% Decrease Compared to 2019 [press release].

https://www.nps.gov/seki/learn/news/sequoia-and-kings-canyon-national-parks-hosted-1-2-million-visitors-in-202 0-35-decrease-compared-to-2019.htm

National Parks Service. (2021). Redwood Frequently Asked Questions. https://www.nps.gov/redw/faqs.htm

NASA. (2022). World of Change: Global Temperatures. Earth Observatory. https://earthobservatory.nasa.gov/world-of-change/global-temperatures

NASA. (2020). NASA Ozone Watch. Goddard Space Flight Center. https://ozonewatch.gsfc.nasa.gov/monthly/monthly_2020-09_SH.html

Nyffeler, M.; Şekercioğlu, Ç.H.; Whelan, C.J. (2018). Insectivorous birds consume an estimated 400–500 million tons of prey annually. The Science of Nature, 105 (7-8). https://link.springer.com/article/10.1007/s00114-018-1571-z

Odion, D.C., Hanson, C.T., DellaSala, D.A., Baker, W.L., & Bond, M.L. (2014). Effects of Fire and Commercial Thinning on Future Habitat of the Northern Spotted Owl. The Open Ecology Journal, 7, 37-51. https://benthamopen.com/contents/pdf/TOECOLJ/TOECOLJ-7-1-37.pdf

Organization for Economic Co-operation and Development. (2012). OECD environmental outlook to 2050: the consequences of inaction - key facts and figures. OECD.https://www.oecd.org/env/indicators-modelling-outlooks/oecdenvironmentaloutlookto2050theconsequencesofinactio n-keyfactsandfigures.htm

Parisi, A.V., Kimlin, M.G., Wong, J.C.F., & Wilson, M. (2000). Diffuse component of solar ultraviolet radiation in tree shade. Journal of Photochemistry and Photobiology B: Biology, 54(2-3), 116-120. https://www.sciencedirect.com/science/article/abs/pii/S1011134400000038

Parks, S.A., Dobrowski, S.Z., Shaw, J.D., & Miller, C. (2019). Living on the edge: trailing edge forests at risk of fire-facilitated conversion to non-forest. Ecosphere, 10(3): e02651 https://esajournals.onlinelibrary.wiley.com/doi/full/10.1002/ecs2.2651

Pennisi, E. (2022, January 31). Rare and ancient trees are critical to a healthy forest: Two studies pinpoint the need for forest diversity in age and species. Science.https://www.science.org/content/article/rare-and-ancient-trees-are-key-healthy-forest#:~:text=%E2%80%9CAncie nt%20trees%20are%20an%20irreplaceable,homes%20in%20 them%2C%20he%20says.

Petek, G. (2022). The 2022-23 Budget: Wildfire and Forest Resilience Package. Legislative Analyst's Office. https://lao.ca.gov/reports/2022/4495/wildfire-forest-resilience-012622.pdf

Petit, J.R., Basile, I., Leruyuet, A.,...& Kotlyakov, V. (1997). Four climate cycles in Vostok ice core. Nature, 387, 359-360.https://doi.org/10.1038/387359a0

Phillips, A.M., St. John, P., Serna, J., Kohli, S. & Newberry, L. (2018). California fire started as a tiny brush fire and became the state's deadliest. Here's how. Los Angeles Times. https://www.latimes.com/local/california/la-me-camp-fire-tictoc-20181118-story.html

Precipitation. (2019). OEHHA. California Office of Environmental Health Hazard Assessment. https://oehha.ca.gov/epic/changes-climate/precipitation

Pugmire, L., Gorman, A., & Weinstein, H. (2003, November 2). Arson Cases Tough to Prove, Even Tougher to Prosecute. Los Angeles Times. https://www.latimes.com/archives/la-xpm-2003-nov-02-me-firearson2-story.html

Purdue Landscape Report: How do trees use water? (2021). Purdue University Extension - Forestry and Natural Resources. https://www.purdue.edu/fnr/extension/purdue-landscape-report-how-do-trees-use-water/

Rice, D. (2017). Study: People start 84% of U.S. wildfires. USA Today. https://www.usatoday.com/story/weather/2017/02/27/wildfires-human-lightning-caused/98480888/

Riddle, A.A. (2019). Timber Harvesting on Federal Lands. Congressional Research Service. https://sgp.fas.org/crs/misc/R45688.pdf

Ritchie, H., and Roser, M. (2018). Ozone Layer. OurWorldInData. https://ourworldindata.org/ozone-layer

Rivers, M., Newton, A. C., Oldfield, S., & (2022). Scientists' warning to humanity on tree extinctions. Plants, People, Planet, 1– 17. https://doi.org/10.1002/ppp3.10314

Robbins, J. (2015, October 9). Deforestation and drought. The New York Times. https://www.nytimes.com/2015/10/11/opinion/sunday/deforestation-and-drought.html

Robbins, Z., Xu, C., Aukema, B.H.,...& Scheller, R.M. (2021). Warming increased bark beetle-induced tree mortality by 30& during an extreme drought in California. Global Change Biology, 28(2), 509-523. https://doi.org/10.1111/gcb.15927

Rosenberg, K.V., Dokter, A.M., Blancher, P.J.,...& Marra, P.P. (2019). Decline of the North American avifauna.Science, 366(6461), 120-124. DOI: 10.1126/science.aaw1313

Ryeol Na, H., Heisler, G.M., Nowak, D.J., & Grant, R.H. (2014). Modeling of urban trees' effects on reducing human exposure to UV radiation in Seoul, Korea. Urban Forestry & Urban Greening, 13(4), 785-792. https://www.sciencedirect.com/science/article/abs/pii/S1618866714000661

Saatchi, SS., Harris, N.L., Brown, S.,...& Morel, A. (2011). Benchmark map of forest carbon stocks in tropical regions across three continents. Proceedings of the National Academy of Sciences, 108(24), 9899-9904. https://doi.org/10.1073/pnas.1019576108

Saliga III, R., & Skelly, J. (2013). Using Chicken Manure Safely in Home Gardens and Landscapes. University of Nevada, Reno Extension. https://extension.unr.edu/publication.aspx?PubID=3028

Sánchez-Bayo, F., Wyckhuys, K.A.G. (2019). Worldwide decline of the entomofauna: A review of its drivers. Biological Conservation, 232, 8–27.https://www.sciencedirect.com/science/article/abs/pii/S0006320718313636

Schick, T., & Burns, J. (2020). Despite what the logging industry says, cutting down trees isn't stopping catastrophic wildfires. Oregon Public Broadcasting. https://www.opb.org/article/2020/10/31/logging-wildfire-forest-management/

Scripps Institution of Oceanography. (n.d.). FAQ: Climate Change in California. Scripps Institution of Oceanography.UC San Diego. https://scripps.ucsd.edu/research/climate-change-resources/faq-climate-change-california

Scientific Assessment of Ozone Depletion: 1998. Executive Summary. (1998) World Meteorological Organization. https://csl.noaa.gov/assessments/ozone/1998/executivesummary.pdf

Sheffield, A., & Kalansky, J. (2022). California-Nevada Drought Status Update. Drought.gov. https://www.drought.gov/drought-status-updates/california-nevada-drought-status-update-6-23-22

Shrivastav, P., & Prasad, M., Singh, T.B.,...& Dantu, P.K. (2020). Role of Nutrients in Plant Growth and Development.Contaminants in Agriculture, 43-59. https://link.springer.com/chapter/10.1007/978-3-030-41552-5_2

Schwartz, M. (2005). Selective logging causes widespread destruction, study finds. Stanford News. https://news.stanford.edu/news/2005/october26/select-102605.html

Siegal, E. (2017). The Terrifying Physics Of How Wildfires Spread So Fast. Forbes.https://www.forbes.com/sites/startswithabang/2017/09/06/the-terrifying-physics-of-how-wildfires-spread-so-fast/ ?sh=3c21ad067791

Smith, D., Hanson, C., and Koehler, M. (2019, October 2). Logging drives carbon emissions from U.S. forests, escalating climate crisis. Missoula Current. https://missoulacurrent.com/logging-carbon-emissions/

Song, H., Wignall, P.B., & Dunhill, A.M. (2018). Decoupled taxonomic and ecological recoveries from the Permo-Triassic extinction. Science Advances, 4(10). https://www.science.org/doi/10.1126/sciadv.aat5091

State of California. (2020). California, U.S. Forest Service Establish Shared Long-Term Strategy to Manage Forests and Rangelands. Office of Governor Gavin Newsom. CA.gov. https://www.gov.ca.gov/2020/08/13/california-u-s-forest-service-establish-shared-long-term-strategy-to-manage-fo rests-and-rangelands/

State of California. (2015). Governor Brown Takes Action to Protect Communities Against Unprecedented Tree Die-Off. Office of Governor Edmund G. Brown Jr. CA.gov. https://www.ca.gov/archive/gov39/2015/10/30/news19180/index.html

Specific Effects of UVB Radiation on Plants. (2022). Climate Policy Watcher. https://www.climate-policy-watcher.org/ultraviolet-radiation-2/specific-effects-of-uvb-radiation-on-plants.html

State of the World's Trees. (2021). BGCI. https://www.bgci.org/wp/wp-content/uploads/2021/08/FINAL-GTAReportMedRes-1.pdf

Steig, E. (2004, December 22). How do we know that recent CO2 increases are due to human activities? Actual Climate: Climate science from climate scientists.https://www.realclimate.org/index.php/archives/2004/12/how-do-we-know-that-recent-cosub2sub-increases-are-d ue-to-human-activities-updated/

Stephenson, N.L., Das, A.J., Condit, R.,,...& Zavala, M.A. (2014). The rate of tree carbon accumulation increases continuously with tree size. Nature, 507, 90-93.https://www.nature.com/articles/nature12914

Sterman, J.D., Siegel, L., & Rooney-Varga, J.N. (2018). Does replacing coal with wood lower CO2 emissions? Dynamic lifecycle analysis of wood bioenergy. Environmental Research Letters, 13(1) https://iopscience.iop.org/article/10.1088/1748-9326/aaa512

Sternberg, L., Moreira, M., Martinelli, L.,...& Nepstad, D. (1997) Contribution of transpiration to forest ambient vapor based on isotopic measurements. Global Change Biology, 3(5), 439-450. https://onlinelibrary.wiley.com/doi/abs/10.1046/j.1365-2486.1997.00082.x

Stidham, M., Toman, E., McCaffrey, S.M., & Schinder, B. (2011). We are improving an inherently stressful situation: the role of communication during wildfire evacuations. Proceedings of the second conference on the human dimensions of wildland fire. Gen. Tech. Rep. NRS-P-84. U.S. Department of Agriculture, Forest Service, Northern Research Station: 96-103. https://www.srs.fs.usda.gov/pubs/38522

Stokstad, E. (2019). Twice as many plants have gone extinct than birds, mammals, and amphibians combined.Science. https://www.science.org/content/article/twice-many-plants-have-gone-extinct-birds-mammals-and-amphibians-co combined

Strahan, S. E., & Douglass, A. R. (2018). Aura Microwave Limb Sounder observations determined the decline in Antarctic ozone depletion and lower stratospheric chlorine. Geophysical Research Letters, 45, 382– 390. https://doi.org/10.1002/2017GL074830

Substantial Antarctic Ozone Hole in 2021. (2021). NASA Earth Observatory.https://earthobservatory.nasa.gov/images/149010/substantial-antarctic-ozone-hole-in-2021#:~:text=Aura's%20Mic rowave%20Limb%20Sounder%20also,to%20shrink%20in%20mid%2DOctober.

Sugar, A. (2000). The long-term impacts of clear-cut logging on insect communities in northeastern Ontario's boreal mixed wood forests. [Masters Thesis, Faculty of Forestry, University of Toronto].chrome-extension://efaidnbmnnnibpcajpcglclefindmkaj/https://tspace.library.utoronto.ca/bitstream/1807/14115/1/ MQ53456.pdf

Swaffar, W. (2016). California's Forests and Waters: An Uncertain Future. National Forest Foundation.https://www.nationalforests.org/our-forests/your-national-forests-magazine/californias-forests-and-waters-an-unce retain

Sweeney, D. (2020, September 29). Glass Fire burned 1 acre every 5 seconds in California. How fast can wildfires grow? The Sacramento Bee. https://www.sacbee.com/news/california/fires/article246092930.html#:~:text=Winds%20topping%2070%20mph %20in,speed%20up%20when%20going%20uphill

The Editors of the Encyclopaedia Britannica. Permian extinction. (2022) Britannica. https://www.britannica.com/science/Permian-extinction

The human fingerprint in global warming. (2015). Skeptical Science. https://skepticalscience.com/print.php?r=109

The State of the World's Forests. (2020). FAO and UNEP. https://www.fao.org/documents/card/en/c/ca8642en

Thomas, S.C., & Winner, W.E. (2002). Photosynthetic differences between saplings and adult trees: an integration of field results by meta-analysis. Heron Publishing. Tree Physiology, 22(2-3), 117-127 https://pubmed.ncbi.nlm.nih.gov/11830408/

Top 20 Largest California Wildfires. (2022). CAL Fire. https://www.fire.ca.gov/media/4jandlhh/top20_acres.pdf

Tran, L. (2021, June 30). NASA satellites see the upper atmosphere cooling and contracting due to climate change. National Aeronautic and Space Administration.https://www.nasa.gov/feature/goddard/2021/nasa-satellites-see-upper-atmosphere-cooling-contracting-climate-cha use

Trees and the Hydrological Cycle. (n.d.) Amazon Aid Foundation.https://amazonaid.org/resources/about-the-amazon/the-hydrological-cycle/

U.C. Davis. Biological Carbon Sequestration. (2021). U.C. Davis. https://www.ucdavis.edu/climate/definitions/carbon-sequestration/biological

United Nations. (2022, May 9). Climate: World getting 'measurably closer' to 1.5-degree threshold. United Nations News: Global perspective Human stories. https://news.un.org/en/story/2022/05/1117842

United Nations. (2022). International Day of Plant Health, 12 May. Food and Agricultural Organization of the United Nations. https://www.fao.org/plant-health-day/en

United Nations. (2015). Paris Agreement. United Nations. https://unfccc.int/sites/default/files/english_paris_agreement.pdf

United Nations Climate Change Conference. (2021). Glasgow Leaders' Declaration on Forests and Land Use. UN Climate Change Conference UK 2021. https://ukcop26.org/

United Nations Environment Programme. (2016). About Montreal Protocol. United Nations Environment Program. https://www.unep.org/ozonaction/who-we-are/about-montreal-protocol

United States Department of the Interior. (2022, April 20). Fuels Management. U.S. Department of the Interior. Office of Wildland Fire. https://www.doi.gov/wildlandfire/fuels

United States Department of Interior. (2020). Budget Justifications and Performance Information Fiscal Year 2021. The United States Department of Interior. Wildland Fire Management. https://www.doi.gov/sites/doi.gov/files/uploads/fy2021-budget-justification-wfm.pdf

United States Environmental Protection Agency. (2022, June 30). Greenhouse gas emissions from a typical passenger vehicle. United States Environmental Protection Agency. https://www.epa.gov/greenvehicles/greenhouse-gas-emissions-typical-passenger-vehicle#:~:text=typical%20passen ger%20vehicle%3F-,A%20typical%20passenger%20vehicle%20emits%20about%204.6%20metric%20tons%20of,aro und%2011%2C500%20miles%20per%20year

United States Environmental Protection Agency. (2016). Climate Impacts on Water Resources. U.S. E.P.A. Climate Change Impacts. https://19january2017snapshot.epa.gov/climate-impacts/climate-impacts-water-resources_.html United States Fish & Wildlife Service. (2021). U.S. Fish and Wildlife Service Proposes Delisting 23 Species from Endangered Species Act Due to Extinction. U.S. Fish & Wildlife Service. https://www.fws.gov/press-release/2021-09/us-fish-and-wildlife-service-proposes-delisting-23-species-endangeredspecies

United States Forest Service and CAL FIRE. (2019). News Release: Survey Finds 18 Million Trees Died in California in 2018. USDA Forest Service. https://www.fs.usda.gov/Internet/FSE_DOCUMENTS/FSEPRD609321.pdf

United States Forest Service. (2019, July 2). Old-growth forests may provide valuable biodiversity refuge in areas at severe fire risk [press release]. USDA Forest Service. https://www.fs.usda.gov/pnw/news-releases/old-growth-forests-may-provide-valuable-biodiversity-refuge-areas-ris k-severe-fire

United States Forest Service. (2017). California Tree Mortality Toolkit. USDA Forest Service. https://www.fs.usda.gov/detail/catreemortality/toolkit/?cid=FSEPRD565838

United States Forest Service. (2017). Drought and Tree Mortality in the Pacific Southwest Region. USDA Forest Service. https://www.fs.usda.gov/psw/topics/tree_mortality/california/documents/DroughtFactSheet_R5_2017.pdf

United States Forest Service. (2016, December 12). California | PNW Research Station. USDA Forest Service. https://www.fs.usda.gov/pnw/taxonomy/term/438

United States Forest Service. (n.d.). General Tree Marking Guide. United States Forest Service. https://www.fs.usda.gov/Internet/FSE_DOCUMENTS/stelprd3794596.pdf

United States Forest Service and the State of California. (2020). Agreement for Shared Stewardship of California's Forests and Rangelands [MOU]. https://www.gov.ca.gov/wp-content/uploads/2020/08/8.12.20-CA-Shared-Stewardship-MOU.pdf

United States Geological Survey. (2018, June 12). Evapotranspiration and the Water Cycle. Water Science School. United States Geological Survey. https://www.usgs.gov/special-topics/water-science-school/science/evapotranspiration-and-water-cycle

Velders, G. J., Ravishankara, A. R., Miller, M. K., Molina, M. J., Alcamo, J., Daniel, J. S., … & Reimann, S. (2012).Preserving Montreal Protocol climate benefits by limiting HFCs. Science, 335(6071), 922-923. http://science.sciencemag.org/content/335/6071/922.

Villar, N., Paz, C., Zipparro, V., Nazareth, S., Bulascoschi, L., Bakker, E. S., & Galetti, M. (2020, November 23). Frugivory underpins the nitrogen cycle. Functional Ecology, 35(2), 357-368. https://doi.org/10.1111/1365-2435.13707

Vincent, M. (2010). Indigenous burn control a myth: study. ABC Science. https://www.abc.net.au/science/articles/2010/12/06/3085726.htm

Voiland, A. (2010). UV exposure has increased over the last 30 years but has stabilized since the mid-1990s. NASA's Goddard Space Flight Center. Phys.org. https://phys.org/news/2010-03-uv-exposure-years-stabilized-mid-1990s.html

Vose, J., Clark, J.S., Luce, C., & Patel-Weynand, T. (2016). Effects of drought on forests and rangelands in the United States: a comprehensive science synthesis. USDA Forest Service, p. 289 https://www.fs.usda.gov/treesearch/pubs/50261

Wagner, D. L., Grames, E. M., Forister, M. L., Berenbaum, M. R., & Stopak, D. (2021). Insect decline in the Anthropocene: Death by a thousand cuts. Proceedings of the National Academy of Sciences,118(2): e2023989118 https://www.pnas.org/doi/10.1073/pnas.2023989118

Wang, J.A., Randerson, J.T., Goulden, M.L., Knight, C.A., & Battles, J.J. (2022). Losses of Tree Cover in California Driven by Increasing Fire Disturbance and Climate Stress. AGU Advances, 3(4): e2021AV000654 https://agupubs.onlinelibrary.wiley.com/doi/10.1029/2021AV000654

Welch, C. (2020, May 28). The grand old trees of the world are dying, leaving forests younger and shorter. National Geographic.https://www.nationalgeographic.com/science/article/grand-old-trees-are-dying-leaving-forests-younger-shorter

Welch, K.R., Safford, H.D., & Young, T.P. (2016). Predicting conifer establishment post-wildfire in mixed conifer forests of the North American Mediterranean-climate zone. Ecosphere, 7(12): e01609 https://esajournals.onlinelibrary.wiley.com/doi/10.1002/ecs2.1609

Weston, P. (2020, December 26.) Mass die-off of birds in south-western US 'caused by starvation.' The Guardian. https://www.theguardian.com/environment/2020/dec/26/mass-die-off-of-birds-in-south-western-us-caused-by-s starvation

Which trees provide the most oxygen over a year, deciduous or evergreen? (2020). CBC News. https://www.cbc.ca/radio/quirks/oct-17-coronavirus-and-pain-sampling-an-asteroid-intersex-moles-and-more-1.57 63905/which-trees-provide-the-most-oxygen-over-the-course-of-a-year-deciduous-or-evergreen-1.5763915

Whitlock, C., Higuera, P.E., McWethy, D.B., & Briles, C.E. (2010) Paleoecological Perspectives on Fire Ecology: Revisiting the Fire-Regime Concept. The Open Ecology Journal, 6, 6-23. https://citeseerx.ist.psu.edu/viewdoc/download?doi=10.1.1.711.7495&rep=rep1&type=pdf

Why Thinning Forests is Poor Wildfire Strategy. (n.d.) Western Watersheds Project.https://westernwatersheds.org/gw-poor-wildfire-strategy/

Wildfire Communications Advisory. (2021). Federal Communications Commission.https://www.fcc.gov/wildfire-communications-advisory

Witze, A. (2005). Antarctic ozone hole set to take 60 more years to recover. Nature. https://doi.org/10.1038/news051205-9

World Wildlife Fund. (2020). Living Planet Report 2020 - Bending the Curve of Biodiversity Loss. World Wildlife Fund. https://f.hubspotusercontent20.net/hubfs/4783129/LPR/PDFs/ENGLISH-FULL.pdf

World Wildlife Fund. (2019). Forest Wildlife Populations have declined by 53% Since 1970. World Wildlife Fund.https://www.worldwildlife.org/stories/forest-wildlife-populations-decline-53-since-1970#:~:text=The%20first%2De ver%20global%20assessment,number%20of%20forest%20species%20live

Wuerthner, G. (2020) Indigenous Burning: Myth and Realities. Rewilding Earth. https://rewilding.org/indian-burning-myth-and-realities/

Xia, Y., Hu, Y., Zhang, J., Xie, F., & Tian, W. (2021). Record Arctic Ozone Loss in Spring 2020 is Likely Caused by Pacific Warm Sea Surface Temperature Anomalies. Advances in Atmospheric Sciences, 38, 1723-1736. https://doi.org/10.1007/s00376-021-0359-9

Zoological Society of London and World Wildlife Fund. (2016). Living Planet Index. Living Planet Index. Zoological Society of London and World Wildlife Fund. https://livingplanetindex.org/data_portal

Zurich, E. (2022, July 7). Ozone Destruction Over North Pole Produces Weather Anomalies Across the Entire Northern Hemisphere. SciTechDaily.https://scitechdaily.com/ozone-destruction-over-north-pole-produces-weather-anomalies-across-the-entire-norther n-hemisphere/

CATRIONA GLAZEBROOK

Catriona Glazebrook led national and international environmental programs for over two decades. She founded Resilient Forests and has researched and applied sustainable forestry practices focused on biodiversity for over three decades.

Catriona served as executive director of one of the largest conservation organizations in the United States. She managed the Gulf Coast sanctuary stretching over 600 miles with wintering grounds & stop-over sites for 98% of the long-distance migratory bird species in N. America. Her program was awarded the Blue Ribbon in Conservation by the Governor and led, in part, to the comeback of endangered species.

Catriona oversaw an international program supporting over 200 environmental organizations and scientists in the US, China, Russia, and Japan. She also worked with international leaders to launch an international conference: "Sustaining the Bering Sea: An International Conference for Collaboration," attended by policy leaders, scientists, local fishermen, NGOs, and indigenous leaders from five countries with a stake in managing one of the most productive fisheries in the world. The conference's outcome was a united international forum that addressed present threats to the health of the Bering and suggested solutions.

The former Vice President of Taiwan invited her to provide environmental leadership for the Democratic Pacific Union, which had a long-term goal of forging a "Union of Pacific Democracies" composed of regional governments to promote democracy, sustainable development, and oceanic culture to benefit the Pacific Region.

Catriona has a Master of Science in Resource Management & Administration and a Juris Doctorate. She began her career specializing in environmental law for seven years. She represented clients before federal and state courts and provided pro bono representation for community groups seeking to protect their local plant and animal species.